Cultivating
STEM
Identities

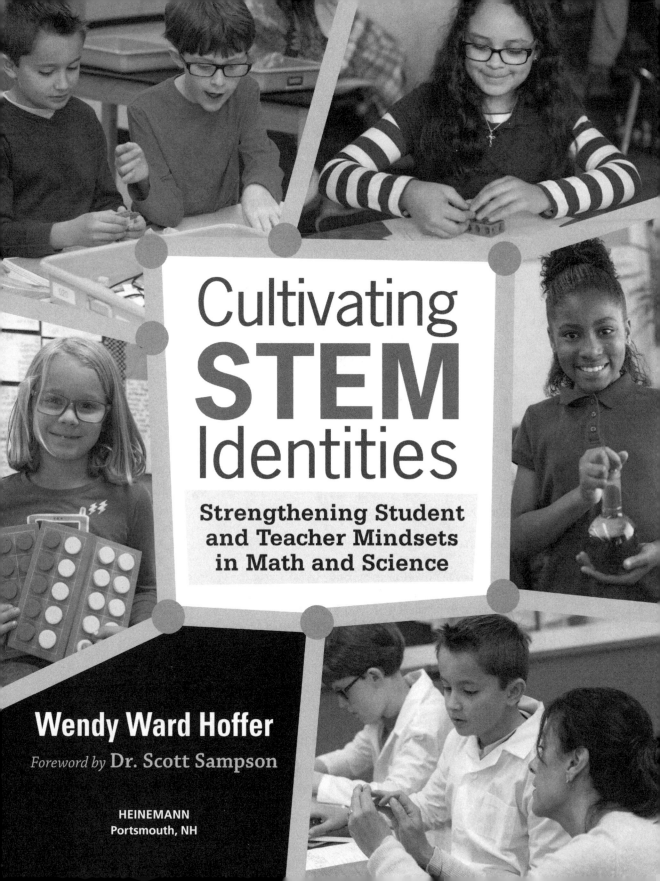

Cultivating
STEM
Identities

Strengthening Student and Teacher Mindsets in Math and Science

Wendy Ward Hoffer

Foreword by **Dr. Scott Sampson**

HEINEMANN
Portsmouth, NH

Heinemann

361 Hanover Street

Portsmouth, NH 03801–3912

www.heinemann.com

Offices and agents throughout the world

The author and publisher wish to thank those who have generously given permission to reprint borrowed material:

Excerpts from the Common Core State Standards © Copyright 2010. National Governors Association Center for Best Practices and Council of Chief State School Officers. All rights reserved.

Library of Congress Cataloging-in-Publication Data
Name: Hoffer, Wendy Ward.
Title: Cultivating STEM identities : strengthening student and teacher mindsets in math
    and science / Wendy Ward Hoffer.
Description: Portsmouth, NH : Heinemann, 2016. | Includes bibliographical references.
Identifiers: LCCN 2016017799 | ISBN 9780325078205
Subjects: LCSH: Science—Study and teaching (Elementary). | Math—Study and teaching (Elementary).
Classification: LCC LB1585 .H59 2016 | DDC 372.35/044—dc23
LC record available at https://lccn.loc.gov/2016017799

Editor: Katherine Bryant
Production editor: Sonja S. Chapman
Cover and interior design: Suzanne Heiser
Cover and interior photos: Laura Mahony Photography
Typesetter: Kim Arney
Manufacturing: Steve Bernier

Printed in the United States of America on acid-free paper

20   18   18   17   16   EBM   1   2   3   4   5

For my God-sent godfather,

Dr. William McNeamer Harvey,

who always reminds me of my true identity

The creation
of a thousand forests
is in one acorn.

—Ralph Waldo Emerson

Contents

Acknowledgments

For catalyzing the development of my STEM identity, I would like to thank my mother, who left us alone to discover in the backyard; my father, who took us to the basement of his UCLA lab to show us what happens when you throw dry ice into a toilet; my stepmom, for teaching us to speak properly about our learning; the beach, for being a place of wonder and change; the group leader from my seventh-grade trip to Yosemite Institute, whose name I don't remember but who invited me to think about why some trees lose their leaves and others don't, and applauded my flawed but hard-thought theory.

For supporting me in myriad ways in all my professional endeavors, I appreciate the thriving learning community of the Public Education & Business Coalition. In particular, I thank Rosann Ward for her leadership and kindness; Lori Pidick for her grant writing collaboration; Traci Lacheta for embossed chocolates; Natalie Newton for unembossed chocolate; Denise Powell for consistently helpful practical advice; the entire PLT—Michelle Morris Jones, Joyce Joyce, Moker Klaus-Quinlan, Kristie Krier, Nancy Meredith, Scott Murphy, Annie Patterson, and Dana Sorensen—for inspiration and thought partnership; PEBC's STEM field staff—Sarah Berger, Jeff Cazier, Emily Quinty, Tracey Shaw, Sathya Wandzek, and Laurie Wretling—for creativity, insight, and good company on the road; the Boettcher Teacher Residency staff, mentors, and residents, past and present, for their dedication to the profession; as well as PEBC's whole operations team—Mindy Armbruster, Caroline Craig, Craig DeLeone, Rose Hagood, and Melissa Kircher—for their grace in keeping the gears greased in so many important ways.

For influencing my thinking about STEM identities, I am grateful to Amber Ptak and the Gill Foundation's Gay & Lesbian Fund for their generous support of PEBC's STEM Mentor's program; to PEBC's 2014–15 STEM Mentors, Ashley Bromstrup, Rachel Gardner, Carrie Halbasch, Kate Klaver, Jeffrey Lewis, Erika Lopez, Caitlin Moore, Amber Myers, Andrea Overton, Tami Thompson, and Shannon Umberger, and their students and schools for welcoming us into their learning communities; to Sarah Berger, my collaborator; as well as to veteran PEBC lab hosts Michelle DuMoulin and Rachel Rosenberg. Most of the vignettes in this book are drawn from these exemplary teachers' classrooms.

I appreciate my numerous conversations with friends and colleagues reflecting on STEM identity; for their particular insights, I am grateful to Robin Koenigsburg, Brad McLain, Daniel Reinholz, and Glen VanBrummelen.

For supporting this project from start to finish and guiding it to publication, I appreciate my editor, Katherine Bryant, and the Heinemann team.

Most importantly, I would like to thank the children—all children—those with whom I live and play, those whose schools and classrooms I visit, those I have yet to meet. Their curiosity and creativity inspire me every day.

And lastly, you, dear reader: I am delighted that you care enough about our future to read this book. I hope that both your own and your students' STEM identities will prosper as a result.

Foreword

My elementary school backed up onto a forest, a green wonderland ideal for igniting young imaginations. One day after school in seventh grade, I was out bushwhacking with my buddy Tim when we happened upon an ancient, half-buried Coke bottle, the surface worn and opaque. We dug around and discovered more exotic items—an old can, a rusted chunk of metal, even a possible arrowhead. Our excitement skyrocketed.

The next morning we ran into the classroom, breathless to tell our teacher, Mr. Duncan, about this major discovery. After school he happily trekked with us to the "dig site," and spent some time poking around the cultural flotsam and jetsam. Eventually he declared, "I think you boys have stumbled upon some sort of old dumping ground. Great job!" Needless to say, Tim and I wore beaming smiles as we hiked back to the school.

The following week, Mr. Duncan announced that the entire class would be headed outdoors into the schoolyard to conduct a mock archaeological dig. We tumbled out onto a low, grassy hill around the flagpole to find several jumbled piles of objects—stuff like cups, bowls, burnt wood, and chicken bones. Each pile, or "site," was divided up into layers separated by paper towels or chunks of sheets.

We kids formed groups of three to "excavate" our archaeological site, carefully recording our findings, making diagrams, and analyzing the results. Eventually it became clear that each layer had different kinds of artifacts, and that we could use these patterns to generate hypotheses about the changing cultures that lived there long ago. Most of all, we were entranced by the joy of discovery.

Mr. Duncan was one of those rare gems of a teacher characterized by broad knowledge, high expectations, and a strong sense of caring. You worked to excel in his class because, well, the thought of letting him down was all but inconceivable.

This remarkable teacher also utilized hefty doses of creativity and hands-on activities, long before educators used terms like "experiential" and "inquiry-based learning." I had no idea at the time (though I'll bet he did), that Mr. Duncan was helping all of us seventh graders forge our own "positive STEM identity"—growing the scientist in each of us.

Most elementary school teachers, then and now, take a more traditional, didactic approach to science teaching. And no wonder. The bulk of these teachers lack any formal scientific training. So it's natural to feel intimidated by the content, and unsure of how to present it. In such situations, the tendency to go into default mode and stick closely to the textbook is entirely understandable. Yet the result, too often, is unengaged learners who get turned off by science.

It is with great pleasure, then, that I welcome you to *Cultivating STEM Identities*. Within these pages, Wendy Hoffer offers up an antidote, an intervention, aimed at breaking the negative chain described above. Wendy is an education expert, particularly passionate about teaching STEM—science, technology, engineering, and math. Within these pages she provides you, the teacher, with easy-to-use tools that will enable your science teaching to be more creative, more engaging, and more experiential.

Also offered up is a provocative array of strategies aimed at building strong STEM identities in elementary school students. Wendy shows how key teacher beliefs (for example, "We are all scientists.") can cascade into teacher behaviors, which in turn directly impact the experience and, ultimately, the identity of the learner.

Assessment after assessment of formal education demonstrates that huge numbers of kids— with a strong bias toward girls, children of color, and those from lower income families—lose interest in STEM fields during the elementary school years. Tragically, that vibrant sense of wonder so prevalent in early childhood is all too often extinguished by the time adolescence arrives. As a result, many, perhaps most, of these children will forge a negative STEM identity that will have cascading effects throughout their lives.

Nevertheless, a large and ever-growing literature, much of it documented in this book, shows that educational interventions focused on quality STEM teaching can make a huge difference. In short, teachers have the power to turn this trend around and help foster the next science-minded generation. Doing so is critical not only for the health of children, but also for the places they live. Indeed, without such a profound shift, things look dire indeed.

We happen to live at arguably the most pivotal moment in 200,000 years of human history. Decisions made and paths taken over the next generation will have reverberating effects throughout Earth's biosphere for thousands, perhaps millions, of years to come (trust me on this; I'm a paleontologist). We desperately need to foster a generation that is science literate. Wrapped up in this idea is the notion of health literacy, environmental literacy, and sustainability literacy. Equally critical is keeping that sense of wonder alive and thriving.

So dig into this book. Then, dip back into it often, particularly when you need a new tool, a new approach, or just a little inspiration. You will quickly find that your confidence and competence with STEM gets a major boost, closely followed by that of your students. As an elementary school teacher, know that you are engaged in some of the Great Work of our time. Warm thanks for your efforts. And enjoy the journey!

—Scott D. Sampson

Introduction

Education has no higher purpose than preparing people to lead personally fulfilling and responsible lives. For its part, science education—meaning education in science, mathematics and engineering—should help students to develop the understandings and habits of mind they need to become more compassionate human beings able to think for themselves and face life head on.

—American Association for the Advancement of Science, Project 2061

Astronaut Mae Jemison, speaking at the Colorado Education Initiative's 2015 annual luncheon, described the need for diversity among medical professionals: not long ago, when oncology was predominated by men, the treatment of choice for breast cancer was radical mastectomy, and with limited success. Meanwhile the male-dominated field had virtually licked testicular cancer without a mention of castration as a treatment option. Now that more women have entered the medical profession, breast cancer outcomes have improved dramatically, and a patient with this diagnosis is far more likely to receive a lumpectomy and radiation than the more dramatic surgery of yore. Who our scientists are matters.

And yet even today, in the wake of the civil rights movement, the equal rights movement, Title 9, and a host of affirmative action efforts, most fields of science, technology, engineering, and mathematics in this country—a collection known by the acronym STEM—continue to be dominated by white men, and generally those from families of means. Don't get me wrong; I love white men. I gave birth to one. Still, all of us will benefit when the doors to opportunity in the STEM fields are flung wide open to all children, of all races, all sexes, all socioeconomic status levels. Just as there was a shortage of research on women's health when men significantly dominated the medical and neuroscience professions (Robert Wood Johnson Foundation 2011), we lack insight into diverse economic, statistical, and scientific issues when the fields of professional mathematics and science are predominantly populated by folks of the same gender and ethnicity. Improving access to STEM careers for people of all backgrounds will not only increase their individual opportunities for economic advancement, offer off-ramps from cycles of poverty and underachievement, but also benefit our collective society by opening doors to new realms of creativity and problem solving.

Kids make up their minds early on—some researchers say by age eight—about their relationship with the fields of math and science, and so, as elementary educators, we are well poised to influence learners' opinions of themselves and these content areas (Weinburgh 1998). Each of us, by virtue of who we are and what we model for children, has the power to cultivate children's optimistic associations with math and science, as well as their positive perceptions of themselves as engineers and problem solvers.

What Is a STEM Identity?

We each have many identities—racial identity, professional identity, sexual identity, our role within a family—all these aspects of ourselves form who we are. Some components of our identity can bring us great joy, as in, "I love being a mom when you let me sleep past 5:30 a.m.," while others can cause us to struggle against discrimination or limiting beliefs, as in "Girls can't be astronauts." (Mae Jemison, of course, proves that wrong, but nonetheless, we swim among some challenging cultural beliefs about girls' opportunities in the STEM fields.) Our identities are informed by our upbringing, our experiences, and society at large, and can shift across time either unconsciously or through deliberate effort.

I have a friend who was not a morning person; in fact in college she had a bumper sticker that stated, "Not a morning person doesn't even begin to cover it." That was her identity when it came to sleep schedules; yet upon arriving in adulthood, with a real job that started at 8:00 a.m., she found the need to revise her identity. With improved sleep management and changes in diet and exercise, she intentionally reset her biological clock. She now relishes mornings and awakens each day before her children to enjoy the smells and sounds of dawn, an intentional identity change from night owl to morning person.

How you think of yourself as a scientist, technology user, engineer, or mathematician is your STEM identity. (We'll get into more detail about STEM identities and the factors that shape them in Chapter 1.) Whoever you are, wherever you came from, whether you love troubleshooting Internet access glitches or hate doing your own taxes, your STEM identity has a hold on you. Similarly, each of your students walks into your classroom each year with a STEM identity all her own, forged through her early life experiences.

What Is STEM?

The acronym STEM is employed in various circles with a range of definitions. Typically, it means merely the collection of the fields of science, technology, engineering, and mathematics. And it is a hot topic.

Some use the term to mean the intersection and confluence of two or more of these traditionally distinct areas of study; others refer to STEM as the application of knowledge from these fields to real world contexts, as in "problem-based" learning. In essence, each of these four STEM fields could be described as using knowledge to solve problems; this is their common denominator. For the purpose of this book, STEM means the content knowledge, as well as the habits of mind, employed by learners in each field.

Stop and Think

- How would you describe your STEM identity?

- How has your STEM identity impacted the trajectory of your life?

You work with young children. You know they are innately curious: they want to rip apart a broken blender to see what's inside, to watch a pair of crickets "do it," to stick their own finger in a mousetrap just to confirm that it will actually snap. Ouch.

"Why did that happen?"

"How did they make it do that?"

"Why does it hurt?"

"Why would you do that to a little mousey?"

"Why aren't you explaining faster?"

"Why?"

Their very nature is as inquirers: research reports that preschoolers ask their parents one hundred questions a day, while middle schoolers ask virtually none (Bronson and Merryman 2010). How can we shift this trend and ensure that all students sustain their innate inquisitiveness and develop identities as curious, productive problem solvers? STEM identities can be intentionally cultivated. This is a book about why they ought to be and how we each can serve learners collectively and society as a whole by creating opportunities for students to be and see themselves as capable and successful scientists and mathematicians. First, let's examine why we must.

Why STEM Identity Matters

The authors of the 2013 Federal Science, Technology, Engineering, and Mathematics (STEM) Education Strategic Plan based their efforts on a growing demand for a prepared STEM workforce, a need to increase our nation's international competitiveness, and the hope of creating a more just and inclusive society. Excellent rationale.

In addition to that committee's strong and familiar arguments about economic development and equality, I would like to add my own four reasons that we ought to prioritize engaging all children's deep investment in their own STEM education: health, opportunity, survival, and joy.

Strong STEM Identities Promote Good Health

While for our society as a whole, life expectancies continue to extend and opportunities for medical care expand, each individual's own health literacy is a significant predictor of her ability to maintain a healthy lifestyle, obtain health services, and comply with doctors' recommendations. According to the U.S. Department of Health and Human Services, only 12 percent of American adults possess proficient health literacy, and thirty million Americans have health literacy described as "Below Basic" (U.S. Department of Health and Human Services 2015). Individuals with limited health literacy—typically those with less than a high school education and folks with limited English proficiency, a disproportionate number of whom are people of color—are less likely to access preventative care, more likely to endure chronic conditions, experience high rates of hospitalization, struggle with low health status, and remain trapped in a cycle of shame that persistently limits their access to the care they need (U.S. Department of Health and Human Services 2015).

While medical professionals make increasing efforts to communicate in plain language and provide access to health care information in accessible formats, all of us are well served to believe in ourselves as capable of understanding the basic principles of human biology and disease. When an individual is met with an unexpected diagnosis, his stress will be less if he and his family members feel confident in their ability to communicate and understand conversations with health care providers. Like fresh water, a positive STEM identity is a basic ingredient contributing to the health of individuals and families.

Strong STEM Identities Open Doors to Opportunity

This is America. You can be anything you want to be, but what do you want to be? The futures children envision for themselves are limited by the scope of their creativity and confidence and the opportunities and encouragement provided by their communities. Given limited awareness, low interest, lax support, and/or lagging self-assurance, many of those traditionally underrepresented in STEM fields continue to sit outside. Statistics on both course and career selection indicate that we are far from achieving gender and racial parity in the STEM fields.

In addition to strong STEM backgrounds creating opportunities for individuals, diversity among the professionals in STEM fields creates greater richness and opportunity for society as a whole. As described earlier, when our scientists, engineers, and doctors fully represent all sectors of society, their research and development will explore the vast interest and needs of humanity's diversity, creating greater opportunity for the health and well-being of all.

Individuals' belief in themselves as capable STEM thinkers, learners, and problem solvers directly impacts the courses they choose and the careers they select.

Strong STEM Identities Increase the Odds of Our Species' Survival

The world is in a fix. Even the Pope is chiming in on climate change. While Dr. Scott Sampson, the paleontologist of "Dinosaur Train" fame, explains that we ought not to introduce apocalyptic topics before fourth grade (Sampson 2014), the reality is that our children are inheriting an imperiled earth.

With environmental challenges more complex than computer modeling can predict, consumerism depleting Earth's resources at an ever-increasing rate, and economic disparities widening the gap between the world's wealthy and those struggling to survive, the future will surely present our children with challenges requiring both STEM solutions and ethical judgment.

As Bill Bryson (2003) describes;

> ". . . if you were designing an organism to look after life in our lonely cosmos, to monitor where it is going and keep a record of where it has been, you wouldn't choose human beings for the job.
>
> "But here's an extremely salient point: we have been chosen, by fate or Providence or whatever you wish to call it. As far as we can tell, we are the best there is. We may be all there is. It's an unnerving thought that we may be the living universe's supreme achievement and its worst nightmare."

Who Participates in STEM?

- The National Science Foundation's 2012 Science & Engineering Indicators showed that in K–12 settings, males are six times as likely to enroll in engineering courses (Figure I.1), and that significant achievement gaps in both math and science persist between different ethnicities and socioeconomic status levels: the achievement of black, Latino, and Native American students, and those from low-income families, was significantly below that of their Anglo, Asian, and more affluent peers (National Girls Collaborative Project 2015).

- According to the National Science Foundation's 2015 report, "Women, Minorities, and Persons with Disabilities in Science and Engineering," 57.3 percent of all bachelor's degrees were awarded to women, yet they received only 18 percent of those awarded in computer science, 19 percent of those awarded in engineering and 19 percent of the physics degrees. Only 11.2 percent of bachelor's degrees in all science and engineering fields were awarded to minority women, followed by a mere 4.1 percent of doctoral degrees in those same fields to minority women in 2011 (Figure I.2).

- Similar disparities follow in the STEM workforce: only 25 percent of mathematicians and computer scientists are women, and only 13 percent of engineers, according to the 2014 National Science Foundation Indicators. And Hispanics, blacks, and Indians/Alaskan Natives comprise only 10 percent of the workers in science and engineering fields, while they comprise 26 percent of the U.S. workforce (National Girls Collaborative Project 2015) (Figure I.3). Economic disparities follow: STEM jobs pay 26 percent higher wages than non-STEM jobs, on average. According to the 2012 census report, there were 7.6 million STEM workers in the U.S., representing one in eighteen workers (Langdon et al. 2011). These jobs are projected to grow by 17 percent from 2008 to 2018, compared to only 9.8 percent growth for non-STEM occupations.

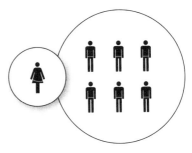

Figure I.1 Female/male enrollment in engineering courses in 2012

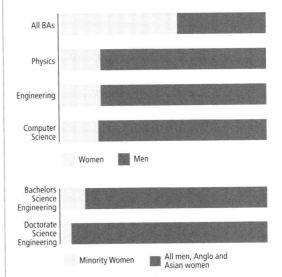

Figure I.2 Degrees awarded in 2011

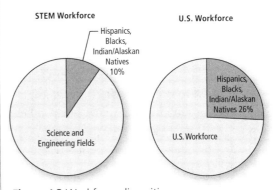

Figure I.3 Workforce disparities

We best equip our children to meet the unforeseen tests and respond to yet unposed questions by ensuring that each possesses a strong sense of herself as capable of making sense, weighing and making decisions based on STEM information as well as the dictates of her own conscience.

Strong STEM Identities Promote Joy

The authors of our Constitution believed in each individual's unalienable right to "life, liberty, and the pursuit of happiness," and to this third end, the pursuit of STEM can provide a prodigious pathway.

Health, wealth, and survival aside, STEM brings joy: marvel at a butterfly wrestling its way out of a cocoon. Watch a gathering storm as the clouds reorganize themselves above your head. Take heart in the magnificence of modern medicine capable of extracting by Cesarean a child who only a century ago would have lost his life and taken his mother's with him. Videoconference with someone on the other side of the world as though they were in the next room. Our children will take these wonders and innovations for granted unless we model for them an appreciation for the intricate beauty of the natural world and point out that our grandparents or great-grandparents had to wait weeks for letters from the front of World War II, to learn only after patient prayers that their loved ones lived.

Stop and Think

- What do you see as the benefits to having a positive STEM identity?
- What are your hopes for your students' STEM identities?
- How will you plant those seeds?

Technology is phenomenal. Nature is brilliant. Rushing through our lives, we can lose sight of the magnificence evident in each moment. A focus on STEM engages our curiosity, beckons us to marvel, to ask questions, to cultivate childlike wonder, and alongside that a pursuit to understand. This is the joy of STEM.

About This Book

This introduction invited you to reflect on why STEM identity is important. Chapter 1 asks you to consider your own STEM identity, the forces that crafted it, and your associated beliefs. From there, each chapter will introduce a productive belief about STEM and describe how that belief can be enacted through intentional teacher behaviors and student learning experiences to support learners' STEM identity development.

- Chapter 1: We Teach Who We Are
- Chapter 2: Beliefs: We Are All Scientists
- Chapter 3: Mindsets: Scientists Persevere
- Chapter 4: Community: Scientists Are Interdependent
- Chapter 5: Content: STEM Is Interconnected

- Chapter 6: Tasks: Scientists Grapple

- Chapter 7: Thinking: Scientists Are Thinkers

- Chapter 8: Workshop: Understanding Takes Time

- Chapter 9: Assessment: Scientists Share

While this book is about STEM identity, I use the shorthand "scientist" to refer to one who engages with STEM, since the fields of technology, engineering, and mathematics can all be collected under the banner of science. Science as the overarching heading for the complex and interrelated studies known as STEM was proposed by the American Association for the Advancement of Science's Project 2061 in their publication *Science for All Americans* (1989). This interesting resource, which offers an overview of the content and history of scientific endeavor, includes chapters on "The Nature of Science," "The Nature of Mathematics," "The Nature of Technology," and "The Designed World." So, with no intended disrespect for any of the discrete but interwoven STEM fields, for the purpose of this text, we will call the explorers of each "scientists."

As I worked to pull the content of this text apart into chapters, I felt as though I were trying to separate one big bowl of spaghetti into separate small portions: all the strands were connected, and when I tried to pull one out alone, I found it tangled up in the rest, all of which wanted to come along. The challenges for you, then, as a reader, will be to patiently savor each portion, or chapter, knowing that it is inextricably linked to all the others in the text. To illustrate this, cross-references are provided throughout, and I made an effort to avoid repetition and redundancy. The good news about this giant portion of spaghetti is that you don't have to eat it all at once: taking any concept in this book, any chapter, and working to implement those ideas into your planning and instruction will have a ripple effect across all other aspects, catalyzing adjustments at a number of levels. The Appendix in the back offers you some resources that may be helpful as you move forward. Be gentle with yourself as you consider change; begin with something bite-sized, and soon learners' whole experience might shift.

About Me

I had the good fortune to come into this world as the daughter of a British scientist. From the time he was fifteen, my dad spent 80 percent of his time studying chemistry, physics, and math and knows more science than anyone I have ever met. He raised us on the beliefs that science was interesting, problem solving was fun, and it is cool to know a lot of obscure information by heart. That was before the Internet.

As I made my way in the world, I learned and taught math and science in many contexts, inside the classroom and out. Most notably, I worked as a specialist for elementary-level classrooms as a garden-based science teacher (as you will read in Chapter 5). Later, after receiving my master's degree in science education, I taught math and science in two of Denver's Expeditionary Learning (EL) schools at a time when EL meant breaking and remaking the mold of public education. With abundant freedom and quite a few tears, I learned by trial and error what does and does not support student engagement and understanding.

For more than a decade, I have enjoyed working with the Denver-based non-profit Public Education & Business Coalition (PEBC), where I now serve as Education Senior Director. My work includes playing the roles of staff developer for schools and districts throughout the nation; math and science methods instructor for our pre-service Boettcher Teacher Residency; workshop designer and facilitator of our Science Institute, Math Institute, Numeracy Institute, and other offerings; as well as author of books for educators about teaching for understanding. Most recently, I have had the opportunity to work closely with a number of inspiring elementary level STEM classroom teachers, PEBC's STEM Mentors, as they honed their craft and reflected on their and their students' STEM identities. Much of the learning I share in this book is a product of that project.

In my work supporting pre-service and in-service teachers, I have struggled to find literature that is both research based and accessible and that merges what we know about science as a way of knowing, teaching for understanding, and content-area literacy for a STEM teacher audience. In response, this is the fourth of my books on pedagogy; my previous works include: *Science as Thinking* (Heinemann 2009), *Minds on Mathematics* (Heinemann 2012), and *Developing Literate Mathematicians* (National Council of Teachers of Mathematics [NCTM] 2016). Though each of these texts targets a unique audience and aspect of instruction, together they stand on common principles:

- We and all of our students are capable mathematicians and scientists.

- Every child deserves high quality STEM education that respects, generates, and challenges thinking.

- Teachers are the best-hearted and hardest-working segment of our population and deserve to be honored and supported as such.

Whatever your STEM story up until now, I am delighted that you picked up this book. I know you became a teacher because you want the best for every child, and yet your plate is full. I am right there with you. Yet cultivating STEM identities does not need to be one more thing to cram into your already overloaded days. It can be the red thread that runs through them, the fuse that sparks student engagement, makes learning experiences meaningful, and inspires delight for all.

CHAPTER 1

We Teach Who We Are

| Teacher Belief | Teacher Behavior | Learner Experience | Learner Identity |

"I look at an awful lot of leaves. I look at them and I ask questions. I start by looking at the color: Exactly what shade of green? Top different from the bottom? Center different from the edges? And what about the edges? Smooth? Toothed? . . .

"Now you ask a question about your leaf. You are now a scientist. People will tell you that you have to know math to be a scientist, or physics or chemistry. They're wrong. That's like saying you have to know how to knit to be a housewife, or that you have to know Latin to study the Bible. Sure, it helps, but there will be time for that. What comes first is a question, and you're already there. It's not as involved as people make it out to be."

—Hope Jahren, *Lab Girl*

Central Question: Who am I as a STEM learner, and why does that matter?

"When I say, 'What is the square root of 81?'" my science professor dad told my three-year-old self, "You say, 'nine.'" I had no idea what a square root was, but I knew enough to do as he said. When his university buddies would visit, he would tell them, "Check this out, I have a really smart kid!" He would call me over in my footie pajamas and ask, "Wendy, what's the square root of 81?"

"Nine!" I would announce to the consistent delight of all the geniuses in the room. I don't know how many times that happened, but it happened enough that I remember the feeling of being perceived as capable in mathematics (though I did not yet understand what I was talking about). This is my earliest memory of myself as a mathematician, one of being surrounded by adults who believed in me. I never looked back. What started as a family joke lodged a sliver of identity in my mind; my actual mathematical competence rose to meet their expectations.

Yet for every toddler daughter taught square roots, there are at least as many American kids given contrary messages, "No one needs math." "Everyone hates science." "Girls can't be engineers." "We are just not a technology family." These beliefs, left to fester, seal learners' fates, and may have informed who you are today as a mathematician and scientist.

What? You don't even think of yourself as a mathematician or a scientist?! The truth is you would not be alone: most American adults don't see themselves in that light.

Yet I am here to tell you, we are all scientists, asking questions and making sense of our own worlds every day. Watch a toddler: what will happen if I tip this cereal bowl? How about if I throw my sippy cup? Experimenting constantly to learn about how the world works. That curiosity and drive for sense making is innate to all of us, yet sometimes school persuades us that science is about memorizing or math is about being quick with calculations. Instead, I invite you to think of all the STEM fields as about inquiry and problem solving—something you do every day.

Who we are and how we orient toward these content areas is a critical first ingredient in supporting students' success as STEM learners. You are indeed a scientist, a mathematician, an engineer, and a technology creator and user, and in this chapter we will explore how you can fully embody that identity, both for your own sake, as well as for your students'.

Stop and Think

- What is your earliest memory of yourself as a mathematician or a scientist?

- What messages did you receive or infer?

- How have those messages impacted the trajectory of your life?

You Are Powerful

Most elementary teachers have earned their teaching license with very little in the way of mathematics or science preparation, and some even admit to being attracted to this profession because of the low math requirements. Over one-third of elementary teachers surveyed lacked full confidence in their own qualifications to teach science (Market Research Institute 2004).

"Many elementary school teachers are anxious about their math and science skills and do not teach them well because of this" (100Kin10 2015). 100Kin10, a nationwide network of academic organizations, businesses, and agencies linked together in response to President Obama's call to train and retain 100,000 highly effective STEM teachers by 2021, identified elementary level teachers' math anxiety as one of seven Grand Challenges we must overcome as a nation to ensure STEM access for all children. Teachers' math anxiety is directly transmitted to their same-gender students: A study of female first- and second-grade teachers and 117 of their students by Sian Beilock and colleagues at the University of Chicago demonstrated the tremendous power of teacher beliefs on students' attitudes and achievement.

> By the end of the school year . . . the more anxious teachers were about math, the more likely girls, but not boys, were to endorse the view that 'boys are good at math and girls are good at reading.' Girls who accepted this stereotype did significantly worse on math achievement measures at the end of the school year than girls who did not accept the stereotype and than boys overall. (Beilock et al. 2010)

This is but one example of the ways in which teachers' ideas about themselves as learners and the views they hold about a particular content area can impact all their students' across time.

Who we are as teachers informs who our students become: if we model optimism, confidence, and courage about STEM in our classroom each day, students will absorb those. If instead we project fear or reluctance, those messages also register in learners' consciousnesses. Many factors might have deterred any of us from cultivating our own strong STEM identities—stereotypes, bias, cultural expectations, opportunity, and so forth. Yet, it is our duty daily to model STEM courage; our own sureness of and interest in these fields—or lack thereof—is absorbed by our students, virtually by osmosis. Our attitudes and beliefs are important teachers. Who we are informs who our students become.

"But I Never . . . "

Whoever you may have been as a mathematician or scientist in the past, whatever your scars from the high school chem lab, any beliefs you may have absorbed about your limitations in STEM, drop them. Now. They no longer serve you or your students. The world needs you to adopt what Stanford's Dr. Carol Dweck (2006) calls a growth mindset: the confidence that with effort and determination, all things are possible.

In her research about people in all walks of life, Dweck uncovered two distinct ways of orienting to the world: a growth mindset—the belief that intelligence and ability are malleable, the result of our persistence—and a fixed mindset—the idea that smarts and skills are rationed at birth and can never be increased. Across the board, in speaking with business tycoons, celebrities, and star athletes, Dweck found that a growth mindset was a common denominator in their success.

Thomas Edison was a model of the growth mindset: after he succeeded in inventing the light bulb, an interviewer apparently asked him, "I heard it took you one hundred tries to get that bulb to illuminate. What did it feel like to be a failure ninety-nine times?"

Edison replied, "I never failed once. I invented the light bulb. It just happened to be a ninety-nine-step process."

This sort of perseverance is what wiped out polio, put a man on the moon, and brought us the iPhone. When we embrace the cultivation of our own STEM identities as a similarly critical endeavor, leaning in with a growth mindset to overcome all challenges, we are sure to succeed.

Regardless of your prior experience with math and science, regardless of your own achievement in these subjects, no matter what you know or don't know about the intricacies of an atom, you, as a teacher, touching students' lives every day, you have everything you need right now to begin to cultivate a positive STEM identity in every child in your care. This begins with your believing in yourself as an engineer, a mathematician, a scientist.

STEM Identity

My cousin's dad died of cancer when she was still in high school—she became a nurse. A friend grew up on a ranch, one of four brothers—three of them became ranchers. You are a teacher; how many teachers are in your family tree? We are each the product of our upbringing—the people who surrounded us, the education we received, the messages we heard, the opportunities we experienced. Every one of us can look back along the trail of our life and see the ways in which experiences, many likely unplanned, formed our identity.

Similarly, STEM identity can grow or wither based on an individual's circumstances. In exploring the relationship between science identity and learning, Brad McLain in his 2012 doctoral thesis, "Science Identity Construction Through Extraordinary Professional Development Experiences," described,

> If the relationship is positive, the meaning [we make of ourselves as scientists] may take the form of science literacy resulting in science related pursuits, a scientifically informed worldview, or even a science related career. If the relationship is negative, the meaning may take the form of science avoidance or even repulsion resulting in the all-too-familiar refrain, "I'm no good at science and math," often echoed as a badge of honor among children and adults alike. (2012)

As McLain describes, one's perception of oneself as capable, competent, belonging, and potentially successful in a STEM learning experience is a necessary prerequisite to the learning itself. Strong STEM identities must, therefore, be seeded and cultivated in each of us so that we, in turn, can pass those along to all of the learners in our care.

For the purpose of this text, we will define STEM identity as follows:

- Qualities of character of STEM thinkers
- Positive regard for STEM content and STEM learning

Let us consider how we can each cultivate those qualities within ourselves so that those same attitudes and behaviors can be passed on to our students (Figure 1.1).

Figure 1.1 Being STEM

Qualities of character of STEM thinkers

	Do	Don't
Curiosity	Be interested in lots of STEM topics	Feel obliged to know everything
Persistence	Work hard in order to understand	Sacrifice sleep and family time to sharpen your STEM skills
Flexibility	Change your thinking as you learn and synthesize new ideas	Beat yourself up about what you did not know in the past

Positive regard for STEM content and STEM learning

	Do	Don't
Be a STEM learner	Seek new learning opportunities and novel STEM experiences	Get lost in the minutia of the learning; instead, remember the big picture
Be a STEM Teacher	Show that you value STEM by devoting time and attention to STEM instruction	Hold firm boundaries between STEM and humanities; instead, show their interconnectedness
Convey optimism	Discuss STEM discoveries and challenges	Suggest STEM is the only future for all learners

Model Magnificence

Though we may not be in positions to impact the mass media, eradicate poverty, restock the toy shelves, reframe the fixed mindset thinking of adults in learners' lives, or address the multitude of other influences that could undermine our students' STEM identities (which we'll discuss more in the next chapter), we ourselves possess a tremendously powerful opportunity to cultivate our own strong sense of ourselves in STEM so that we can, in turn, foster students' understanding of and confidence in these critical fields.

Summers throughout my college years, I worked at a sleep-away summer camp whose traditions included a morning run and a leap into a not-very-warm lake. For everyone. No exceptions. "I don't care if you are 'not a morning person,'" our boss informed us at staff training one June. "Fake it. That is your job here. If you run, they run. If you jump off the dock, they jump off the dock." He went on to regale us with a true story of a young camper who, several summers ago, his very first morning there, joined the masses leaping into the lake, only to remember moments later, as he landed in the chilly water, that he did not yet know how to swim. (He was promptly rescued.) The point was this: with buoyant enthusiasm, we could compel even nonrunners and nonswimmers to participate in morning exercises with spunk and pizzazz. And so we did.

Let's not make lemmings of anyone, but rather recognize the tremendous opportunity we have as adults, as leaders in learners' lives, to model those behaviors that will catalyze their success. We teach who we are.

STEM Qualities of Character

Later in the text, we will explore the Next Generation Science Standards' Science and Engineering Practices, as well as the Common Core Standards for Mathematical Practice, two thoughtful lists of sixteen features in all that ought to be woven throughout learners' experiences with STEM. Yet for now, let us consider just three critical qualities of character that successful STEM professionals and avid STEM learners alike embody. Here are some ideas as to how you can be a role model for each.

Curiosity

"Being curious makes you powerful." This was the enduring understanding a cross-curricular team at Prairie Middle School adopted for all their students as a yearlong goal. In modeling curiosity for learners, the team focused not on valuing the knowing but rather the process of finding out. This is what mathematicians and scientists do: inquire.

STEM content can be daunting. Concerned that we may not have the requisite background knowledge to understand astrobiology or genetic engineering, we may be tempted to shy away. Yet, if we approach new learning from a stance of curiosity (What questions does this conjure in me?) rather than with a need for quick mastery, we can engage as scientists pursuing understanding through curiosity. Try just listening to a five-minute podcast on a science topic and jotting down as many questions as come to mind. There—you are inquiring. Strong start.

Carve out a little time to dig deeper into your own STEM learning. What are you curious about? Keep a journal and document your thinking and discoveries. Share this with your students as a way to model lifelong curiosity and learning. Though this may feel like one more thing in the face of all the emails you need to respond to and all the lessons you need to plan, the excitement of learning can give us energy and propel us forward in all areas of our lives. Being curious makes you powerful.

Persistence

Education researcher Jim Stigler described a study that illuminated notable cultural differences in our perceptions of struggle: he and his colleagues gave an impossible math problem to groups of first graders in the United States and Japan. He reported, that the American kids, "worked on it less than 30 seconds on average and then they basically looked at us and said, 'We haven't had this.'" By contrast, the students in Japan stayed focused for a full hour on the impossible task, right until the researchers stopped their work and told them the problem was not solvable (Spiegel 2012). He makes the point that these attitudes, inculcated in youth, have a lifelong impact on the trajectory of learners' lives.

Science and engineering are all about failure and tenacity. It took thousands of geneticists

Voices in the Classroom

George rushes to his teacher Ms. Halbasch as first-grade math work time wraps up and his classmates gather on the rug. He quickly thrusts his notebook into her hands. "This actually took me a lot of thinking," he pronounces, and she kneels down to meet him eye to eye.

"Are you worn out?" she inquires.

He nods, "Yes," and smiles.

"As a mathematician myself, I get so excited to see you guys just digging in and sticking with it. How did that feel?"

"Good."

Carrie Halbasch's twenty-five first graders gather in a tight bunch at the front of the room, leaning in to hear their teacher's gentle voice over the murmurs coming through the accordion wall separating them from the class next door. Carrie invites the students to show with their thumbs up, down, or sideways how they felt as problem solvers today. Most students show a sideways thumb, their class' hand gesture representing, "I felt challenged but able to persevere."

"I love it when it feels like this," Ms. Halbasch affirms, showing her own sideways thumb. "When it's a little bumpy, guess what's happening to me as a mathematician?"

"Growing!" the class replies in chorus, familiar with her frequent reminders of the value of grappling with challenges.

Language That Models STEM Character

In modeling all of these qualities of character, we can watch our habits of speech. Use language that communicates confidence and optimism about yourself as a STEM learner (Figure 1.2). Pretty soon you will hear your students doing the same.

Figure 1.2 Shifting to Growth-Promoting Language

Typical	Growth-Promoting
"I was wrong."	"I disagree with myself."
"I don't know."	"I don't know *yet*."
"This is hard."	"I need to persevere."
"I don't get it."	"What questions do I need to ask or answer in order to understand?"

fifteen years to complete the Human Genome Project, cataloguing all 200,000 base pairs contained in the nucleus of every living cell in your body. Perseverance is the substratum of success.

We can model similar persistence in our own lives with relentless pursuit of our passions: what do you love to do and learn about? Share this with students, talk about your hard work and effort and the ways that it has paid off. Describe how this is what scientists and mathematicians do: press on in the face of challenge and adversity. Perseverance pays.

Flexibility

"I disagree with myself," Rachel Rosenberg is apt to confess to her fifth-grade students when she wants to change a mathematical solution or adjust her hypothesis. She does not call herself wrong or bad or dumb, just evolving in her thinking.

Our understanding of math and science is constantly changing, both individually and culturally: humans once thought it impossible to travel place to place by flying through the air, or to speak to friends on the other side of the world while walking along a beach, or to survive influenza. Yet STEM inquiry and STEM learning are constantly changing the landscape of our human experience.

Similarly, we can allow our individual knowledge and understanding to evolve. We begin this process by being okay with not knowing, by grasping ideas loosely and being open to changing our thinking. When we cultivate and model a comfort with the unknown, a willingness to engage with new ideas, and an openness to adjusting our thinking, we show students the reality of what it means to be a STEM learner. As the ancient Greek philosopher Heraclitus put it, "There is nothing permanent except change."

Positive Regard

When we save science for Thursday afternoons at 2:00 and then let the reading block run over, allowing no time to actually get messy with the lab activity, we communicate a low value for STEM learning. When we keep the math manipulatives on a high shelf and only let students engage with them for brief periods during a structured lesson, we communicate that math is separate from our other work as learners. Why not make friends with STEM and let it leak across your days?

You don't have to adore STEM just yet—just start with positive regard, believing in the possibility that it could be lovely. Here are some steps for putting that positive regard into action.

Be a STEM Learner Every Day

Grab a buddy, make a commitment, and start with some small steps. These might include:

- Read a book about an appealing science subject
- Pursue some online math learning
- Take a class or webinar on computer programming
- Find a STEM news source (see appendix), and challenge yourself to read a quick STEM-related article on a regular basis, then to share what you learned with someone in your life.

Catch yourself if you are tuning out when science topics might come up in your world, and instead challenge yourself to tune in. As you stretch in these ways, focus on your mindset, the grit and effort mathematicians and scientists need to succeed. Pretty soon, you will have ample stories to tell your students about how you struggled and persevered—excellent modeling. Remember: be curious.

Be a STEM Teacher Every Day

Make time for STEM. It doesn't have to be an hour-long lesson or a daily hands-on experience—just delve into something for a few minutes that connects classroom learning to the broader world of STEM. This might involve telling a story about mold in your fridge, troubleshooting the Smart Board as a class, sharing about fixing your bicycle, or describing the latest news from the International Space Station. Be excited, and share that enthusiasm with learners.

Consider how you can weave STEM into the rituals and routines of your classroom on a regular basis. These might include you or your students regularly presenting the group with

- mental math challenges;
- technology troubleshooting tips;
- science current events; or
- engineering puzzlers.

We'll look at this in more detail in Chapter 4.

Convey Optimism About STEM Opportunities.

Where are these fields taking us? What will we discover next? Which of the world's problems can

Unanswered Questions

While students will surely have questions of their own to discuss and explore, why not introduce them to some authentic STEM-related inquiries of our day, both scientific and ethical?

- How can we cure cancer?
- How will we meet the growing nutritional needs of an expanding population?
- How can we make transportation more efficient?
- Where should we put our garbage?
- Should we colonize space?
- Should we preserve endangered species?
- Should we clone humans?

Add your own as you learn more about current explorations and discoveries!

we solve? When we discuss with learners the future of engineering and technology, imagining what new inventions may be developed, we invite students to envision themselves in the future. By learning about the lives of individual scientists, their learning and achievements, we offer ourselves—and the learners in our care—role models who can inspire our own STEM identities. Invite learners to dream big.

By embodying the qualities of character of STEM learners and then developing and modeling positive regard for STEM, we can each inspire students to grow their own positive STEM identities.

Conscious Cultivation

The purpose of this book is to offer all elementary level educators an accessible approach to planting the seeds of STEM success in the minds and hearts of young learners. Either consciously or unconsciously, your beliefs about STEM impact your behavior and instruction. These create learners' experiences and thereby their identities. In this book we will explore how you can intentionally support students in developing positive associations with STEM, by configuring your own productive beliefs, by behaving in ways that communicate your beliefs, and by enacting learning experiences that elevate students' sense of themselves as scientists. At the opening of each subsequent chapter, you will see the following graphic, mapping how you can intentionally enact your great faith in and hope for students as STEM learners with specific teacher behaviors that will shape their experiences and impact their identity development.

| Teacher Belief | Teacher Behavior | Learner Experience | Learner Identity |

You have a key opportunity to be conscious and intentional about how you influence your students by your own example.

Let's do some math: if they are with you for 180 days for seven hours a day, and I multiply those two numbers together, that tells me you and your students have—try it in your head—7 times 100 is 700, 7 times 80 is . . . well, 7 times 8 is 56 so 7 times 80 is 560. 560 + 700: that gives you 1,260 hours with your students. Am I right? Please check that for me. I just modeled mental multiplication for you—how I think through a math problem—which I hope inspired your confidence in the partial product method of multiplication. It only took a minute. And 1,260 hours is 75,600 minutes—that is how much time you have with each of your students each school year.

Think of all the modeling you are doing in that time. Here is your opportunity: intentionally grow and cultivate your own STEM identity so that you model for all learners the curiosity, persistence, and flexibility, as well as the positive regard for STEM, that they need to succeed.

CHAPTER 2

Beliefs: We Are All Scientists

Teacher Belief	Teacher Behavior	Learner Experience	Learner Identity
All learners are capable of STEM success.	Hold and model high expectations for all; address stereotypes that arise.	Students recognize and reflect upon the impact of their own and others' beliefs.	I am a STEM thinker.

Each second we live is a new and unique moment of the universe, a moment that will never be again . . . And what do we teach our children? We teach them that two and two make four, and that Paris is the capital of France.

When will we also teach them what they are? We should say to each of them: Do you know what you are? You are a marvel. You are unique. In all the years that have passed, there has never been another child like you. Your legs, your arms, your clever fingers, the way you move.

You may become a Shakespeare, a Michelangelo, a Beethoven. You have the capacity for anything. Yes, you are a marvel. And when you grow up, can you then harm another who is, like you, a marvel?

You must work—we must all work to make the world worthy of its children.

—Pablo Casals (*Joys and Sorrows: Reflections of Pablo Casals*)

Controversy exploded in 2015 when British Nobel Laureate Dr. Tim Hunt addressed the World Conference of Science Journalists. "Let me tell you about my trouble with girls. Three things happen when they are in the lab: you fall in love with them, they fall in love with you, and when you criticize them they cry" (Knapton 2015). Though his comments were apparently taken out of context, what is a woman or a girl to infer about her place in science when words like these fall from the lips from an esteemed researcher at the top of his field?

While great strides have been made over the last century to open opportunities to folks of all backgrounds and diversify the STEM workforce, unproductive beliefs still hinder prospects for many potential scientists and engineers.

STEM Beliefs

Our beliefs about STEM as a body of knowledge, as a learning process, and as a community of learners inform our beliefs about our own STEM identity. In this chapter we will explore how stereotypes, biases, and misconceptions about the nature of STEM, unaddressed, can fester into unproductive beliefs—and what we can do to intentionally reverse these trends.

Cultural Stereotypes

Who are scientists? Antisocial geeks with pocket protectors? As rational adults, we know this not to be the case, and yet the stereotype persists: researchers have described our culture as "science-hostile" (Osborne, Simon, and Collins 2003), presenting images of scientists and engineers in a negative light and promoting stereotypes of them as socially awkward know-it-alls. These images serve as a particular deterrent to girls and traditionally underrepresented minorities who may be interested in pursuing these fields.

In her recent *Atlantic* article, "The Stereotypes That Distort How Americans Teach and Learn Math," Stanford Professor Jo Boaler explains:

> . . . the idea that math is hard, uninteresting, and accessible only
> to "nerds" persists. This idea is made even more damaging by harsh
> stereotypical thinking—mathematics is for select racial groups and men.
> This thinking, as well as the teaching practices that go with it, have
> provided the perfect conditions for the creation of a math underclass.

Stop and Think

- Where do you experience or observe STEM stereotypes?

- How have STEM biases impacted your life?

- What sorts of messages do you notice your students receiving from the media about STEM content, STEM professionals, and who belongs in those field?

- How does your school—through policies, programs, or teacher beliefs—support all learners' STEM confidence and competence?

Narrow mathematics teaching combined with low and stereotypical expectations for students are the two main reasons that the U.S. is in dire mathematical straights." (Boaler 2013)

Popular media is alive with messages that promote negative or biased stereotypes about STEM professionals and about who belongs in STEM fields, and casts impressions of these content areas as difficult and uninteresting. A few pink Lego sets and a handful of mathematical mystery-solving shows on TV have not yet impacted this cultural belief: a recent study by Dario Cvencek at the University of Washington Institute for Learning and Brain Science found that by second grade, students had internalized the stereotype that math was for boys, and the boys in this study identified themselves more closely with mathematics than their female peers (Cvencek, Meltzoff, and Greenwald 2011).

Stereotype threat—an individual's awareness that she is not expected to perform well because of a cultural belief about her gender or ethnicity—is also demonstrated to impact students' performance. When children as young as six were asked to perform an academic task they perceived to be an assessment, and in an area where they perceived their identity group to typically underperform, they fared far worse than when the task was presented in a nonevaluative framework (Desert, Preaux, and Jund 2009). Assessments, therefore, may show us far more about what students believe about themselves than about what they are actually capable of doing.

STEM stereotypes are alive and well in America; they move into our minds and throughout our culture almost invisibly, tainting the flavor of our thoughts. Yet, when we pause and unpack them, shedding the light of truth on erroneous beliefs, they lose their power over us. How can we work with students to deconstruct stereotypes that may already have taken root in their young minds?

Deflating Stereotypes

A first step in replacing stereotypes with productive beliefs is to ferret them out in our own minds and to replace them with the confident conviction that we are all scientists. Say it. "We are all scientists. Science and math and engineering are for everyone." How does that feel? You have to believe it in order to teach it. Once we get our own consciousness straightened out, we can then address stereotypes that learners may be voicing or experiencing or enacting, and next invite them, hand in hand with us, to approach the unfortunate biases of society at large.

Voice and Model Your Beliefs

So often, our beliefs are the invisible ingredient in our interactions, yet this need not be the case. You can level with kids about yours: tell them often that they are all scientists and mathematicians; explain how curiosity is their very nature; highlight the good sense they come in with every day and how those qualities of ingenuity innate in each one of them will make them excellent engineers. When you call learners together to gather on the rug, call them what they are, "Today, scientists, we are going to explore . . . "

Each time you see learners interacting in ways that demonstrate the qualities of character of successful scientist, you can remind them by noticing and naming those behaviors (Figure 2.1).

Figure 2.1 Notice and Name Nonstereotypical Behavior Aligned with Productive Beliefs

Productive Beliefs	Notice and Name Behavior
We are all mathematicians.	"I see every mathematician getting started solving this problem!"
Science is for everyone.	"Scientists share. I love how Ava and Quintin are taking turns with the hand lens."
Scientists persevere.	"You know what I noticed about Henry's work today is that even when he got stuck, he did not give up."

Now, I know teachers of even our youngest have heard their students voice stereotypical beliefs ("Math is for geeks."), or seen them behave in stereotypical ways (a girl relinquishing control of science equipment to a boy in the group). When these instances occur, we need to stop and address them. Without shaming or blaming, we can simply notice, inquire, and respond with true, antistereotype statements (Figure 2.2).

As you begin to watch and listen with greater attention, you may be dismayed to notice how frequently unconscious stereotypes bubble up in the form of student behavior. Let go of feeling like you need to police and respond to every possible act. Every teacher learns to pick her battles, so when it comes to STEM identity, seek to seize those teachable moments, to gently draw them to the attention of the group at large, and to use them as opportunities to surface, examine, and respond to inequities and stereotypes.

One teacher attending to stereotypes around STEM noticed that the Lego area in her first-grade classroom was constantly swarmed with boys during choice time. She decided to bring this up in her class meeting. She started by inquiring, "How many of you like Legos?" Nearly all the students put up their hands. From there, they launched into a discussion about how even though everyone likes Legos, it seems to be all boys at the classroom Lego table. Learners shared their thinking on why this had become the trend and then problem-solved ways to offer more equal access. They decided to revise their choice time agreement to state that on Mondays and Tuesdays, the Lego table was for girls only; on Wednesday and Thursday, it was for boys, and on Fridays anyone could play there. While this may seem sexist to segregate a toy or area

Figure 2.2 Address Stereotypical Behavior by Noticing, Inquiring, Informing, and Seeding Change

When we see/hear	We might say . . .			
Stereotypical Behavior	Notice	Inquire	Inform	Expect Change
Student states she can't do the work because, "Math is for boys."	"I heard you say, 'Math is for boys.' . . ."	"Why might you think that?"	"Well, that is interesting, but that is not what I think. I know a lot of girls who love math. In fact, it was a woman named Ada Lovelace who developed some of the first mathematical understandings that led to modern computers. Let's find out more about her, shall we?"	"How can you get yourself started on this task?"
A child of color is being sidelined while white children dominate at an engineering task.	"I see that you boys are doing most of the building and talking and that Donovan has not yet really gotten involved."	"Why is that?"	"Do you know how important it is that we have engineers of all backgrounds and ethnicities build the cities of the future? We need everyone in this group to have an equal chance to grow their thinking."	"Donovan, what do you need in order to feel more included?"

of the classroom by gender, the teacher found that many girls who in the past had perhaps been intimidated by a large group of boys at the Lego table now opted to participate there on the "girls only" days. Though this was not a research-informed intervention, this single case study demonstrated that when given an intentional invitation and the space to explore safely, learners of any gender embarked on all sorts of new projects and discovered other options because their old habits had been disrupted.

Inquire About and Address Learners' Beliefs

Beyond their observable behaviors, students possess a whole range of beliefs that drive them. Find out what students think about math and science, who they believe works in those fields, and what opportunities they anticipate may be available to each of them as STEM learners. Some sample discussion topics to this end might include the following:

- What is math? What is science? Talk with learners about how math and science are all about problem solving. They are life skills that can serve them no matter what they choose to do in the future. Share real-life examples of problems you solve: how to get to work when your car is in the shop, how to get the stain out of your new jeans, what to do when you don't have an internet connection and need something online.

- Who needs engineering? Who needs to understand technology? Discuss all the ways in which your daily life is touched by human-designed technology. How did you get to school today? Why do the lights go on when we flick that switch? Where did your breakfast come from?

- Who are scientists? Talk about all the different sorts of work professionals conduct in the STEM fields, the great diversity of opportunities available. Invite guests speakers, read profiles of scientists, reach out to professionals in your community, learn from short videos about the work of modern engineers. Think outside the box: the custodian who manages the school's furnace uses scientific thinking every day, as does the landscape worker who selects which plants belong in the shade, or the network engineer who keeps your computers running. Invite each of them in to talk about problems they have encountered and how they solved each. Scientists don't have to be guys in lab coats.

Stop and Think

When you watch how your students engage as STEM learners, do you see them enacting typical cultural stereotypes?

- Do they voice positive regard for themselves as scientists?
- Do they join groups confidently?
- Do they share materials equitably?
- Do they participate fully?
- Do they speak courageously about their ideas?
- Do they listen to and honor all peers' thinking, regardless of gender, race, or other distinguishing qualities?

If no, how might you notice, inquire, inform, and then expect change?

In addition, we can bring in real data about who our scientists are (such as that presented in the introduction of this book), invite learners to look at that data and ask questions, notice trends, talk about why it may be the case that certain professions are dominated by certain groups. Be honest about how this is a concern to you and a problem that can be overcome. Insist that you envision each and every child as a scientist, with great potential in STEM fields in the future, and that they have the opportunity to reverse historical imbalances and inequities.

Talk Back to the Media

Create time for learners to stop and think about media messages. While popular media has become increasingly sensitive about their portrayals, stereotypical messages and anti-STEM propaganda do sneak in. More pervasive are stereotypes about who "belongs" in the STEM fields; computer science and engineering, fields dominated by white and Asian men, continue to be portrayed as such in popular TV shows like "Silicon Valley" and "The Big Bang Theory." And who anchors the popular science show "Mythbusters"? Two white guys.

When we see these media stereotypes in action undermining learners' equitable visions of their own futures, we can catch them and talk back, as did thousands of people in response to Dr. Tim Hunt's comments at the beginning of this chapter. Here's an opportunity to bring literacy and STEM together: invite learners to write to the TV networks or producers or actors, to share some data with them, and let them know why it's important to see STEM represented positively and scientists and engineers portrayed by actors of all backgrounds and genders. Send the letters. People in the entertainment business want attention; they write back.

Teacher and School Bias

A friend of mine, now CFO of a large, successful nonprofit, told me the story of her journey as a mathematician in high school: she was told flat out that she could not take calculus because she was a girl. It was not until a math teacher's son, a fellow student whom she had peer-tutored in math all through the previous year, came to her defense that she was permitted to register for the advanced math course. This is an extreme case of the sort of school and teacher bias that has influenced the trajectory of too many young STEM learners. As I have asked teachers and other adults about their own early experiences with math and science, stories of this nature pour out.

A study by Drs. Victor Lavy and Edith Sand at the University of Tel Aviv identified the relationship between girls' early educational experiences and their later STEM achievement. They explored how teachers' innate gender biases play out: when teachers knew the names and genders of math test takers, they scored boys higher. When the test takers' identities were anonymous, girls actually ended up with higher scores. The study went on to demonstrate the long-term impact of a biased teacher: students whose sixth-grade math teachers showed bias against them were found to score lower in eighth-grade math, as well as to choose fewer advanced math and science courses in high school, sealing their futures outside the STEM workforce (Lavy and Sand 2015).

Though this particular study took place overseas and examined the difference between genders in math, natural inferences can be made about the effect of teacher bias on any subgroup and the long-term impact it can have on learners' future opportunities. I have heard many high-achieving adults tell stories of how their mathematical or scientific aspirations were thwarted by a biased school administration whose policies tracked them into low-level courses, a discouraging teacher who coached them out of a tough science class, a school counselor who steered them away from AP STEM courses, or other unfortunate failures of our system to hold the bar high for every learner and then scaffold her success.

Teacher bias, as well as bias within the school system, limits learners' opportunities. Watch for yours, and jump on it. Here are a few ways to work against bias.

Expect Everyone

When observing teachers' instruction of math and science, I often find myself noticing who gets called on to speak, and in some cases find that the air time is not equally shared between boys and girls, and among students of a global majority. By simply paying attention to who gets to share their solution, who gets to manage equipment, and how we respond to each, we can convey the confidence that all learners are capable and expected to participate and succeed (Figure 2.3). Here are some strategies to try:

- Practice and teach growth mindset. (More on this in Chapter 3.)

- Make a habit of alternately calling on a girl, then a boy, or an English language learner, then a native speaker.

- Keep track of who gets odd jobs or opportunities and pay attention to who gets on that list; find ways to give everyone a chance.

- Intentionally group learners. (More on this in Chapter 6.)

- Invite a peer to observe your class to notice any ways in which you may not be attending to students equally.

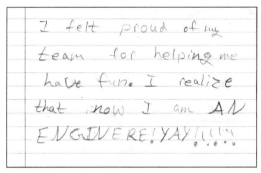

Figure 2.3 Student reflection on engineering task

Promote Equity

While slogans like "Every child—every day," drift by on school buses, the reality is, when it comes to STEM, it will take more than a catch phrase to reverse centuries of prejudice and bias that have left some children out in the cold. We can, through intentional effort, make significant progress in demonstrating our beliefs that we are all scientists. I invite you to look for ways that your classroom and school may be sustaining STEM bias, and intentionally work against those. In your classroom, you might try the following:

- Teach STEM content when everyone is in class, not while certain groups are pulled out for language support, GT opportunities, or other special interventions.

- Experiment with same-gender or same-race groupings, and see what differences students observe in their participation or behavior. Similarly, experiment with mixed groups.

- Ensure equal access to technology, science equipment, and math supplies during choice times; if needed, create systems for turn-taking that ensure access for all.

- Highlight the contributions of little-known STEM heroes from all cultures and genders.

Then take a look schoolwide: Does the after-school robotics club meet at the same time as choir, forcing learners to choose? Are all students encouraged to compete in the science fair? What are your colleagues' beliefs about STEM and STEM identity? Seek to ensure that the doors of opportunity and access to STEM experiences are open to all by starting courageous conversations with colleagues. To this end, you might

- Share with administrators, colleagues, and parents some of the data on the impact of STEM identities;
- Lead a faculty discussion about STEM identities and beliefs;
- Propose a series of walk-throughs or peer observations looking specifically for STEM equity; or
- Assemble an interested group of colleagues to do some action research, test driving interventions that could draw in traditionally underrepresented groups.

Depending on your school, district, and community culture, STEM equity may be a touchy topic, as may be teacher-initiated campaigns of any sort. If this is the case, I suggest starting small, in the domain of your own classroom, and explaining to students and families what you are doing and why. Let folks know these are experiments for which you are gathering data. Welcome their input. Be willing to adjust course and to share your findings.

Stereotypes, biases, and unproductive beliefs are like air: they can drift around our classrooms invisibly, yet permeate all our interactions and experiences. When we intentionally make the invisible visible—or audible—we invite learners to reflect critically on the culture around us and the ways in which it influences our perceptions of ourselves and our opportunities in STEM.

CHAPTER 3

Mindset: Scientists Persevere

Teacher Belief	Teacher Behavior	Learner Experience	Learner Identity
Scientists persevere.	Teach growth mindsets; present challenges and teach strategies to sustain stamina.	Students engage in productive struggle and practice persistence.	I am capable of overcoming difficulties through effort.

Central Question: How can we support STEM learners in sustaining their stamina?

While serving as the only doctor at the National Science Foundation's South Pole station in the winter of 1999, physician Jerri Nielsen discovered a lump in her own breast. With only ice as an anesthetic, she performed a biopsy on herself with the support of a welder she had trained for the job of cosurgeon. (He practiced on a potato and a piece of chicken.) Images from her biopsy transmitted back to the United States revealed an aggressive cancer, yet Nielsen was trapped in Antarctica

If I have the belief that I can do it,
I shall surely acquire the capacity to do it
even if I may not have it at the beginning.

—Mahatma Gandhi

for months because of conditions too cold for an evacuation flight to land. The military airdropped medication, and she treated herself with hormone therapy and chemotherapy injections until she could be airlifted out six months after her diagnosis. She described her experience, "The things that make you strong, and make you feel as though you've accomplished something, are not the easy ones; it's the things you had to work and struggle through. Those are what give us our depth . . . and texture and longing" (Sullivan 2009).

But what if Nielsen had grown depressed, refused to give herself the shots she needed to fight the disease? What if she had lagged in confidence and allowed doubts to overtake her mind, undermine her resolve, drive her mad with fear? Her belief that she had the ability to manage her illness herself under these harsh conditions gave her the strength to persevere in the face of tremendous challenge.

While all learners benefit from the cultivation of growth mindsets, this mindset is particularly important to STEM learners because the very nature of STEM studies requires perseverance in the face of uncharted challenges: engineering is all about designing, testing, and redesigning; scientific inquiry involves experiment after experiment to find the truth; challenging mathematics requires creative problem solving; and every technology user knows that equipment needs troubleshooting on a regular basis. STEM success requires perseverance, and a precursor to perseverance is a growth mindset.

Mindset

As described briefly in Chapter 1, in her research on successful professionals from all walks of life, Dr. Carol Dweck found that those who achieved were those who possessed what she calls a growth mindset, the belief that perseverance is more important than pedigree.

In her book *Mindset*, Dweck juxtaposes a growth mindset with the fixed mindset stance that abilities are innate, and our individual aptitude cannot be changed. Figure 3.1 shows what individuals with each mindset might say about STEM.

As you glance at the descriptors of Dweck's two mindsets, you may see yourself in one column or the other. Picture some of your students and infer their mindsets related to STEM. How do their beliefs about the role of effort relate to their achievement and behavior in class?

Sarah Sparks explains,

> New research suggests students with a more positive "growth mindset" in math have brains that may be more primed for solving math problems. In a Stanford University study, students who scored higher on an assessment of positive mindset have more brain activity throughout

Figure 3.1

Fixed Mindset Beliefs	Growth Mindset Beliefs
• Intelligence and ability are fixed.	• Intelligence is malleable.
• Some people have a math gene, some don't.	• Anyone is capable of succeeding in STEM.
• If you're not a science person, you never can be.	• With hard work, you can grow and learn anything.
• Effort does not matter.	• Effort is the most important ingredient for success.

*several areas associated with math problem-solving, as well as more
efficient connections with the hippocampus, an area associated with
memory recall in math. (Sparks 2015)*

Given the direct impact a child's mindset is demonstrated to
have on her learning and problem-solving ability, it is incumbent
on all teachers to intentionally cultivate growth mindsets—both in
ourselves and among our students. (Note that someone could have a
growth mindset in one area of his life—say, learning to play piano, as
in, "I am going to practice every day for at least thirty minutes until
I master this piece," while holding a fixed mindset in another, "I just
can't do math, and I will never take another math course.")

Celebrating Struggle

While we often see growth-minded thinking in society's successful,
we can find a fixed mindset belief in some of our highest-achieving
students. Having been told all their lives how very clever they are,
some students can develop a sense of responsibility to preserve their
own cleverness. To this end, these "smart kids" may avoid academic
risk taking in order to secure the world's perception that they are
successful students. In this way, a fixed mindset can hold high achievers back.

Struggle is integral to success, not a sign of weakness. Too many
generations of math and science learners came to believe that being
smart meant having all the answers. Yet, professional success in
each of the STEM content areas comes from thinking deeply and
creatively. In order to encourage students to embrace a growth
mindset, we need to reframe their perception of the role of struggle
in learning.

Mindset Is an Invitation, Not a Blame Game

Recent critics of mindset instruction point out that a simple
claim that one's mindset can
ensure success could result in
victim blaming: if a child raised in
poverty, struggling to learn in the
face of trauma and tragedy, could
only embrace a growth mindset,
the world would be his oyster.
That is not what I am suggesting here. Rather, regardless of a
child's background, she is well
served to understand that her
outlook and self-perception can
be intentionally focused toward
those qualities of character demonstrated by research to more
likely foster academic success: a
growth mindset.

Meanwhile, it is incumbent
on schools, teachers, districts,
parents, and communities
to cultivate the conditions
that support all children's
opportunities.

Dweck and her colleagues examined brain scans of individuals engaged in challenging work and were able to prove scientifically that when we grapple with challenges, we actual develop new neural pathways; we get smarter. The brain, like a muscle, needs a regular workout to get stronger. Once students understand this reality, their behavior changes: hard tasks, once avoided, become worthy ones because they make us smarter. When we talk with learners about how their effort makes their brains grow new synapses, they can feel inspired to work hard through confusion. School becomes not about being right, but about learning to think.

In her recent article "Memorizers Are the Lowest Achievers and Other Common Core Math Surprises," Dr. Jo Boaler describes the importance of debunking the myth that math is memorizing and goes on to explain the reality of the subject's complexity,

> *Mathematics is a broad and multidimensional subject. Real mathematics is about inquiry, communication, connections, and visual ideas. We don't need students to calculate quickly in math. We need students who can ask good questions, map out pathways, reason about complex solutions, set up models and communicate in different forms.* (2015)

Science, technology, engineering, and mathematics, by their very nature, require us to stretch to understand ideas, grapple with tough problems, attempt several iterations of a model or solution, and at times dwell in uncertainty. These experiences, familiar to professionals in these fields, can be uncomfortable to the novice who believes that knowing and being first to "get it" are the way to succeed in STEM. By teaching growth mindsets and the value of struggle and effort, we equip learners to persevere through the myriad challenges their adventures in STEM will present.

In order to promote success in STEM—and in all other subject areas, for that matter—a growth mindset is a critical ingredient (Figure 3.2).

Molding Mindsets

I was recently challenged by a student in our teacher preparation program: What if a child has a fixed mindset, but is fine with that? Who are we to try to change them? I believe that it is our duty as teachers to impart both knowledge and character to our students. To that end, consciously cultivating frames of mind that will support learners in meeting their maximum potential is indeed our responsibility. Growth mindset is one such frame of mind that will serve our students and support them in becoming all that they are capable of becoming as mathematicians and scientists—and beyond.

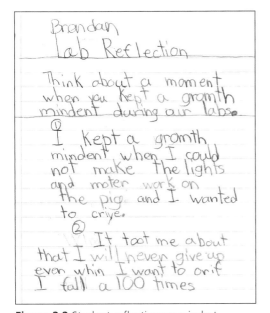

Figure 3.2 Student reflection on mindset

According to education researcher Camille Farrington,

> *Students always have mindsets and they're always in the process of affirming the mindsets they already have. If they believe that they don't belong or they can't really do it then they'll be looking for confirmation that that's true. It's the teacher's job to interrupt that negative mindset and turn it around to something positive and adaptive.* (Schwartz 2014)

So, where might we begin in intentionally cultivating learners' growth mindsets related to their STEM identities? Four suggestions follow:

- explain and model
- present challenges
- teach strategies
- praise carefully

Explain and Model

Now that you understand what the growth and fixed mindsets are, you can describe them to your students. (If you want more background on the research behind them and a thorough understanding of the consequences of each, Dweck's *Mindset* [2006] is a great resource.) After offering an overview, you might invite each learner to think about an area of their life where they have a growth mindset, where they have applied effort and seen improvement. You might also ask them to consider a situation where their mindset might have been fixed, an instance where they insisted that they were unable to do something. Learners can then notice how their mindsets affect their experience.

A critical point for STEM learners is the reality that possessing a growth mindset, being willing to pour effort into learning even when times get tough, benefits them greatly: they will get smarter.

When it comes to math and science, we can point out how common it is to encounter peers and relatives with unproductive, fixed mindsets—beliefs that they can't do math or they don't or won't like science, or that technology is not their friend. We can level with students about the reality that STEM is a part of life. If they want to drive a car, they have to know how to change a tire; want to cook, need to grasp some chemistry; want to raise a family, need to know some basic human biology. Given STEM's pervasiveness and importance, we had best cultivate our growth mindsets and make friends with these content areas as soon as possible.

We might also introduce learners to STEM achievers who demonstrated the qualities of character of growth mindsets: Jonas Salk worked for eight years to develop the vaccine that eradicated polio, one inoculation at a time; 2004 Nobel Prize Winner Wangari Maathai preserved millions of acres by planting one tree at a time, launching Kenya's Green Belt

Voices in the Classroom

After some independent work time on inequalities, fourth-grade math teacher Rachel Rosenberg gathered her students on the rug to debrief. "If you feel pretty good about using some strategies when you got stuck, put your thumb up," she invites. Many thumbs. "What did you use today when you got stuck to help you be successful?"

Students share their strategies, including drawing pictures, asking questions, talking with peers, using tools. Amani describes how she rewrote a confusing problem to make it something she knew how to solve.

Rachel affirms, "Amani, I love how you said to yourself, 'I'm stuck here,' but you didn't give up, did you? You thought about it and tried a strategy and persevered."

Voices in the Classroom

Rachel Rosenberg responds to a fourth grader working hard to add fractions with different denominators, "I love what you are doing. You are doing what a good mathematician does. You are connecting to what you learned before. And do you know what else you are doing? You are showing stamina; that means you are sticking with it. That's what good mathematicians do."

movement; the team at NASA that brought the imperiled crew of Apollo 13 home safely against tremendous odds by solving one problem at a time. When we look at the lives of these achievers and see the obstacles they overcame, we can infer that each possessed a growth mindset and found the inner strength to show stamina in the face of worthy struggle.

In addition to speaking of heroes from other times and other places, speaking of your own mindset can empower learners to shift theirs. Most of your students probably look to you and figure you have everything worked out: your fly is always zipped; you put your shoes on the correct feet without thinking about it; your socks match; you remember your lunch and know where you put your keys—well, most of the time. We grown-ups make it all look easy, so for students it is helpful to hear of times where we ourselves needed to apply effort and persistence in order to succeed. Tell stories from your own life as a growth-minded scientist and mathematician: how you rose to the challenge of completing your own taxes despite your desire to pay someone to do them for you; the cake you baked that flopped at altitude, and how you tried again; the struggles in your garden and how you engineered a system to keep the varmints out; your first days as a teacher, digging deep to manage a classroom of squirrely students who liked to test you.

After you have introduced the growth mindset as a concept, narrate examples from your own life and the lives of others to build learners' schema. Make an intentional effort to notice and name students' growth mindsets and persistence and to acknowledge the strategies they used.

In bringing growth mindsets to life for students, some teachers invite learners to engage in a moment of reflection before facing a challenge to consider what they can do to sustain their stamina that day. "Being a scientist can be challenging. How will you persevere today? What will help you keep yourself going?" Students share marvelous ideas:

"Think positive."

"Ask for help when I get confused."

"Stay with my group even when it's hard."

"When I get frustrated, take a deep breath and come back."

"Remember that when my brain hurts, it's because it's getting smarter."

When students take time to think this over, to set an intention to sustain their perseverance, then share their strategies, they come to understand that a mindset can be nurtured through understanding, awareness, and effort.

Present Challenges

Boaler described how important challenges and open-mindedness on the part of instructors are to cultivating learners' mathematical insight. Contrary to popular opinion, she explains,

> New brain science tells us that no one is born with a math gift or a math brain and that all students can achieve in math with the right teaching and messages. The classrooms that produce high achieving students are those in which students work on deep, rich mathematics through tasks that they can take to any level they want. No one is told what level they can reach and no one is held back by narrow questions that limit students' mathematical development and creativity. (2015b)

Learners pick up on all our cues about our belief in them: one such cue is the sort of work we invite them to do and the scaffolds we do or do not provide. A child consistently offered perplexing puzzles will infer that her teacher believes her to be the sort of child capable of complex work, while a peer handed only rote worksheets might develop a sense that this is all her teacher sees her as able to do. Too often, we offer students easily digestible tasks in order to save them from struggling. And yet the value of productive struggle is consistently determined in educational research.

Some teachers believe that given a choice, students would prefer easier tasks, when in fact, teachers I work with have found the opposite to be true: learners like to challenge themselves, to feel capable. One teacher I know would receive a shipment of leveled vocabulary books from his district each year, with a list of which student, based on their score on last year's state test, belonged in which level book. One year, the list did not come, but the books did, so he let the students each choose their own vocabulary books from the color-coded stacks. Do you know which pile ran out first? The highest-leveled book! Students are hungry to be seen as capable and to be pushed, to do more than what has traditionally been asked of them.

Many schools make a habit of assigning students to "ability" groups, then giving each group a different task based on their perceived ability. What does this suggest to students? Once a bluebird, always a bluebird: fixed mindset. When, instead, we mix the groups, offer learners a choice of challenges from which to select, they can make their own decisions about how to push themselves.

Michelle DuMoulin's first-grade math class was studying in and out boxes— puzzlers where learners were looking at a column of inputs and their outputs and inferring the rule describing what happens to a number when it is put inside the "box." She opened with a minilesson reminding

learners about the big idea of their work, then laid out six different incremental challenges, each on its own sheet of paper. Each team got to choose where to begin: many grabbed for the puzzle with the highest numbers first, while others decided to start in the middle, and a few began with the very simplest problem. As students worked, Michelle conferred and, in some instances, suggested that learners challenge themselves at another level. In this way, she offered learners flexibility and choice, demonstrated a growth mindset about their abilities as mathematicians, and was able to give feedback on their decisions as needed.

Presenting challenges to learners communicates clearly our great confidence in their abilities. In Chapter 6, we will look more deeply at how to design juicy challenges that can promote growth mindsets, STEM understanding and positive STEM identities.

Teach Strategies

When we do raise the bar and ask learners to rise up with greater effort, we need to remain vigilant to their levels of frustration: productive struggle is one thing, but despair is entirely another. They look different: learners engaged in productive struggle are leaning in, asking questions, writing, thinking, puzzling, discussing while despair takes us away to the drinking fountain to dawdle and avoid work (though a walk to the water fountain might be a needed brain break for a diligent learner as well). Last week, I watched a group of students grapple very hard to interpret a challenging graph: first they read silently and annotated their papers, then they discussed it as a group, asking questions and sharing ideas, then they all got silent again, staring at their papers, jotting notes, then looked up and discussed more, and finally agreed to go talk with other groups to see what they were doing. This persistence went on for fifteen minutes, but as an observer I was impressed that no one gave up; they were able to persevere because not only did they have growth mindsets but also they relied on strategies to support their productive struggle.

One basic principle we can promote is the idea that there is nothing wrong with being temporarily "stuck" as a learner, given that one then pursues the means to become "unstuck." Strategies for getting unstuck can include a broad array of resources, materials, tools, classmates, research, and thinking, as well as drawing on one's own internal reserves of resolve. Some teachers take times to chart these and keep them posted in the classroom as a ready reference for mired mathematicians or engineers. Train students to avoid helpless hand raising and instead identify a need and fill it for themselves: model, practice, debrief, and reflect on their efficacy at navigating the stickiness inherent in complex STEM challenges. The following are some suggestions to help learners persevere.

How to Get Unstuck
1. Realize you are stuck.
2. Determine what you need in order to get unstuck (see Figure 3.3).
3. Get what you need. (If you are not sure what you need—ideas, information or resources—get something and see if it helps. If not, try something else.)
4. Take a deep breath and persevere.

Figure 3.3 presents some questions a learner might ask herself.

Figure 3.3 What do I need?

Ideas	Information	Resources
• What is the problem I am trying to solve? • Where have I seen something like this before? • What is the big concept I am working with, and what do I know about it? • What strategies could I use?	• What else do I know? • What questions will I ask? • Where will I find needed information, a reference or a person?	• What tools or materials would help? • Where will I find those?

Related to strategies for getting unstuck, learners also benefit from knowing thinking strategies to support their work as problem solvers. Chapter 5 explores more strategies students can learn to scaffold their own STEM thinking and learning.

When we have a growth mindset, we know that getting stuck is just part of life; everyone's been there; there's no shame in it. When we honor, rather than shy away from, the struggle and have strategies to manage the stress of it, our perseverance flourishes.

Praise Carefully

In a study completed by Dr. Dweck and her colleagues at Stanford, graduate students offered learners a series of puzzles, all the while sitting close by and giving the participants specifically designed feedback. In the first portion of the study, the student subjects, all around age ten, were praised for their cleverness while completing the puzzles, as in, "My, you are quick! Look how smart you are! Wow! The solutions are coming so easily to you! You are really good at this!"

After a series of puzzles punctuated with this sort of praise, the tester then offered the subject an option, something like, "Would you like to do more puzzles such as these, that you will probably get right, or would you like to challenge yourself with some more difficult work that you might learn from?" Overall, those students who had been primed with a fixed mindset—those complimented for being bright—stuck with the easier puzzles.

As part of the same study, with another group of individuals and the same puzzles, another flavor of praise was doled out: "What great effort

Voices in the Classroom

Michelle DuMoulin starts each year teaching first-grade math and science in what she calls her overacting phase. "Do you know how genius it is that you got the hundreds chart today to help you solve that problem? Genius!" She dramatically yet sincerely emphasizes and celebrates small acts of student independence and their own demonstrated abilities to problem-solve. Her message to learners: You have everything you need in this room to be independent. "If they don't get that," she explained to a group of visiting teachers, "they follow you like mice. I need them to know they can do it without me." She spends her entire year building learners' confidence in themselves. "I want them each to say, 'I am a mathematician.'"

you are putting into this work! I love the way you are sticking with it. You are really working hard," and so forth. This growth mindset praise resulted in very different outcomes when the choice point came: when invited to keep doing the easy puzzles or to select tougher ones, this group, primed with a growth mindset, opted for the steeper challenges. It only took a few minutes in every case to indoctrinate a student into understanding what was valued: cleverness or endurance.

Think of all the time you spend with learners each day and of all the opportunities you have to inoculate them with a growth mindset! Intentionally notice and name behaviors that demonstrate a growth mindset and invite learners' self-awareness. To this end, take time to celebrate:

- **Determination:** "Starting over after your first tower tumbled, that shows great determination."

- **Effort:** "I notice you chose to erase and rewrite that sentence so that we can all read it clearly; what great effort you are putting in."

- **Hard work:** "Even though the problem was challenging for this team, they stayed with it and worked hard to find another solution."

- **Perseverance:** "I saw you ready to give up when you found out you had made a mistake in the multiplication, but then you went right back to your table to rework the problem. Way to persevere!"

- **Stamina:** "You kept writing silently for the entire fifteen minutes, and you explained your theory in two different ways with sketches to illustrate. That took a lot of stamina!"

- **Strategies:** "Though at first you weren't sure how to get started, I saw you pull in a lot of resources to support yourself. You got the tens frame, some teddy bears, a new piece of paper. What great strategies!"

- **Thought:** "I noticed you took the time to go back and rethink your plan; you erased and corrected your procedures. What great thought you put into this experimental design!"

When we narrate behaviors that demonstrate productive qualities of character, we illustrate to all learners in earshot what it looks like to embody a growth mindset, increasing the likelihood that each will, in turn, do the same.

In addition to our praise, we can take care in how we respond to learners' vocalizations of their own discouragement. "I can't do it!" one might cry out in frustration at his inability to get his paper boat to float.

"Yet," is all we need to reply. "You cannot do it *yet*." The addition of this one simple word, *yet*, has been picked up even by "Sesame Street" as a critical strategy in promoting growth mindsets among learners bound to struggle who can indeed, through perseverance, succeed. One special education teacher I met told me she has the word *yet* in a very large font on the door to her office, so each person who enters sees it. She points to it as a powerful reminder that though one may not know or be able to do something, that knowledge and ability are just around the corner.

The growth mindset is critical to STEM success; it gives learners insight into the value of struggle and the importance of perseverance. A growth mindset can be intentionally cultivated: once we offer and explain it to students, we can reinforce this mindset through modeling, presenting appropriate challenges, teaching strategies, and praising carefully.

Einstein famously implored us, "Do not worry about your difficulties in mathematics. I can assure you that mine are still greater." Frustration and confusion are part of all learning, and especially STEM learning. When we look our doubts and fears about ourselves and our own abilities in the eye and meet them with the sure confidence of a growth mindset and the certainty that through effort we grow our abilities, we can emerge from struggles, as did Dr. Jerri Nielsen, stronger.

CHAPTER 4

Community: Scientists Are Interdependent

Teacher Belief	Teacher Behavior	Learner Experience	Learner Identity
STEM professionals and STEM learners collaborate.	Create and sustain respectful communities of learners.	Students work effectively and efficiently with all peers.	I am a collaborator. We are smarter together.

It is these undeniable qualities of human love and compassion and self-sacrifice that give me hope for the future. We are, indeed, often cruel and evil. Nobody can deny this. We gang up on each one another, we torture each other, with words as well as deeds, we fight, we kill. But we are also capable of the most noble, generous, and heroic behavior.

—Jane Goodall, *Reason for Hope*

"Find someone you can have a really good math conversation with," third-grade teacher Ashley Bromstrup invites her students. "With your partner, talk about what you know about area and perimeter." Clustered on the rug at the front of the room, students animatedly discuss, gesturing with their hands as they describe various figures.

After a few minutes of enthusiastic paired sharing, Ashley rings her chime for the group's attention, "Hopefully you had a chance to speak with your partner about perimeter and area. These are words we haven't really talked about this year. I am wondering what you remember. What do we know about area?"

Stop and Think

- What is the relationship between community and learning?

- What does it mean to be an interdependent learner?

Laura starts, "Let's just say there is a square right here. All the space inside it is the area."

Ashley records Laura's idea on a large piece of chart paper, then turns to Laura and invites her, "Call on a boy, please."

Tyler shares, "You are in a backyard. Your fence would be the perimeter of your yard, and the garden would be the area. Or an ice rink."

Again, Ashley records, then guides Tyler, "Please call on a girl who is raising her hand patiently and quietly."

Xanthia speaks, "Perimeter is like the edge around the rug, the very outside. The tiny tiny black line, the outline."

"Can you call on a patient, quiet boy, please?"

Colin explains, "Area is kind of like the space inside the perimeter, inside of the perimeter is the space, the area."

A few more learners chime in, and Ashley fills the chart paper with their thinking, then shifts gears: "I want to open up our conversation a little bit more. I am wondering what questions we have about perimeter and area. Looks like we are getting some ideas together about what they could be. But what questions do we have?"

Merrill is quick to hop in, "My question is, does it have to be like a square or can it be a Picachu's tail that has a perimeter? So I am asking if it can be different shapes of perimeter."

Alec asks, "My question is about area. Is area the inside of something or the outside of something?"

Kaya, "Could a perimeter be an area and could an area be a perimeter?"

Piper, "Could perimeter be on something that is 3-D?"

Adam, "My question is, what about the area outside of the perimeter?"

Nolan, "Could the perimeter be on something bigger than a carpet, like something outside?"

Sapphire, "If area gets bigger, does perimeter get bigger?"

Ashley and her students created a chart full of questions and curiosities about the meanings of these concepts—area and perimeter. Throughout their group conversation, Ashley honored learners' thinking by recording their ideas, and offered them agency, the opportunity to self-regulate and call on peers in turn. The questions on the charts they generated drove their community's enthusiastic math work for several weeks.

In visiting classrooms where STEM learners thrive, I observe a palpable energy and joy: students are up on their tiptoes to gaze and point into the terrarium; a child grasps for manipulatives and clicks them quickly to illustrate her solution; learners rush to the rug to share their thinking at the close of a workshop. They get so engaged in a discussion about circuits that no one cares if the bell rings; it's not about recess, it's about understanding important and interesting ideas. Common features to each of these flourishing learning communities include the following:

- Intentional Environments
- Agreements
- Flexible Grouping
- Rituals and Routines

In this chapter, we will explore some options for each.

Intentional Environments

I remember visiting my dad's university lab as a kid: there were big humming machines, lots of tiny glass bottles, labeled petri dishes, some microscopes, and plenty of other equipment I could not name, stacks of paper, and posters of data. The scientists who worked there wore lab coats and goggles and sometimes solemnly moved samples around, at other times laughed their heads off at jokes I did not understand. The whole place smelled like science; nothing else could possibly be going on in there.

Fifth-grade teacher Tami Thompson asked this question: "When people come into my room, how will they know that this is a STEM classroom?" I ask this same question of you: how does your learning environment communicate your beliefs about STEM, the nature of your STEM learning community and what it means to be a STEM learner?

Walls

Who is doing the work? Our classroom walls can answer this question. Use wall space to present evidence of student thinking: collaborative projects, problem solving, visual representations of thinking, and photos of young scientists in action along with their writing about their experiences. You might also choose to post the Big Idea or Essential Question for your unit, along with student writing about each. An interactive word wall can also serve as a rich resource supporting vocabulary acquisition. Commercially produced materials or carefully penned teacher-created charts can be lovely, yet balance those by also displaying your students' hard work and their wonderful ideas, reminding all that this classroom is about learners' thinking.

Materials

"You are a scientist, and you can access the materials scientists need to think and work." This is what our classrooms can say to learners.

STEM instruction can be messy and involve a lot of stuff, no doubt. Every teacher has her own strategies for managing the material chaos that can ensue. Ample storage is a must, whether in the room or down the hall. But for whatever work or projects you are engaged in, make the materials accessible, on low shelves, in containers children can access freely, not stored high in cupboards or considered off limits but for special blocks of time. When we offer children the time and space to explore STEM materials—rocks, rulers, modeling clay, and math manipulatives—we support their STEM identity development.

Time

"You have time to do the important work of exploring and thinking about math and science." This is the message our schedules can send to students in our learning communities.

When do students work on science, math and other STEM subjects in your classroom or school? How does their timing in the day and the time allotted to these studies communicate the value placed on them? Don't save STEM until the end of the day or the end of the week! Use it to jump-start learners' brains and hook their interest. Liven up literacy with a STEM-related reading or writing exercise: these content areas need not be separated. In fact, literacy is integral to STEM learning, and they can feed one another: I have seen reluctant writers seize the pen when invited to document their observation of a robot at work, and a bored reader can get gripped by a nonfiction text on where rainbows come from.

Class Pets

In addition to the typical furnishings of tables and chairs, some STEM teachers add animal habitats to their classrooms: aquariums, terrariums, habitrails, and more. The responsibility to care for critters can catalyze community and cooperation between learners, as well as serve as a source of ownership and pride. Animal friends can create great interest and excitement for students, yet it can be a big job to look after them. Michelle DuMoulin relies on class parents to help her keep her small zoo going; each fall, she explains to the parents, grandparents, anyone else willing to participate that the animals in her classroom are an important part of their learning community, but that she will need parents' help to look after them. She is blessed that each year a posse of volunteers agree to clean cages, pet-sit over holidays, and even provide food and bedding for the animals. Last time I checked, she had a bird, a snake, three tortoises, a baby porcupine, a tank full of fish, and a lobster living in her classroom.

If that all sounds a bit overwhelming, and your students' families are not in position to support a class menagerie, you might take a page from another first-grade teacher's book: her class pets are wood lice, also known as pill bugs. No smell, no noise, just a little tray in a corner. But the students love to watch and feed them all the same.

Agreements

How will we treat each other, ourselves, our equipment, our time as STEM learners? Shared agreements build community. We can intentionally create a classroom culture of mutual respect and collaboration by establishing, modeling, and holding all participants accountable to supportive agreements about how we learn together. You may already have such agreements in place; you may have cocreated those with your students. Wonderful!

In establishing class agreements, some teachers present a prepared list for discussion, others bring in a few ideas and let the students refine and revise those, while the most constructivist start from scratch with the discussion question: what do we need as learners in order to thrive together? Whatever your strategy, time invested up front in developing class agreements aligned with your values and beliefs about being a STEM learning community reaps tremendous payoffs later on.

Figure 4.1 shows a few valuable agreements for classrooms seeking to establish a culture of rigorous STEM learning.

Specific Expectations

In addition to setting norms for students' learning community in general, teacher Tracey Shaw also takes time early in the year to explore with students her expectations for various kinds of learning: individual time, partner time, group collaboration, and whole-group discussion led by the teacher. They devote class time to discussing what each of these forms of participation should look and sound like. She saves the lists from their conversation on slides in her computer, and shares them back to the groups, as appropriate, throughout the year. This investment of time up front buys her a lot of time later in ensuring that students transition and work efficiently, since everyone understands their shared agreements about how scholarly behavior ought to look.

Figure 4.1 Sample Agreements

Agreement	Meaning	Celebrations	Prompts
You are responsible for your own learning and for supporting the learning of others.	You are the boss of yourself, expected to make wise choices that support your learning, including where you sit, who you work near, what materials you choose, how you use your time, and how you respond to adversity. Further, you are expected to work and learn in a way that does not detract from the learning of others, including managing your movement, volume, materials, and focus, as well as balancing your own speaking and listening in conversations.	• I see ____ making a wise choice to ask for help when she is struggling to get online. • I notice ____ choosing a quiet place to finish her work, away from distractions. • I hear ____ taking time to explain her thinking in support of ____'s learning.	• What is your responsibility as a learner right now? • How are you supporting ____'s learning? • What do you need in order to take responsibility for your learning?
Share with humility.	When presenting your thinking with a partner, small group, or in a whole-class discussion, share confidently yet respectfully. Allow time for others to respond and ask questions. Appreciate and respond to their questions as probes to deepen your thinking and understanding.	• I appreciate how ____ concisely explained her work and then invited the group to ask questions. • I respect how ____ described her plan so far and then invited input from peers.	• How do you think you sound to your classmates? • How are you inviting your peers to push your thinking?
Listen with the intent to understand.	When peers or teachers are sharing, focus with your mind and body and work hard to make sense of what they are describing.	• ____ is ready with a question, which shows he has been working hard to understand. • I can see that I have ____'s entire attention because he is facing me with curious eyes.	• How can you show you are listening? • As a listener, what are you wondering?

(continues)

Figure 4.1 *Continued*

Agreement	Meaning	Celebrations	Prompts
No one is done until everyone is done, understands, and can explain.	As collaborators, you need to attend to the learning of everyone in your group: if one person has finished her own task, it is her duty to see how she can support the learning of peers—not just help them complete the work, but truly collaborate until each member of the team understands and can explain.	• This group is deep in conversation, ensuring that all members understand. • I saw ____ work closely with ____ and support her understanding.	• Does everyone understand? • Is everyone ready to explain? • What does your team need in order for everyone to be done?

Flexible Grouping

Scientists and engineers collaborate. There is no possible way anyone could build the Golden Gate Bridge, put a man on the moon, or prevent AIDS alone. We need each other.

Students can achieve more collaboratively than independently (Vygotsky 1978). Yet inviting students to simply "work together" can be only moderately effective; group work serves best when students are assigned rich, groupworthy tasks (see Chapter 6) and are supported in participating equally (Cohen and Lotan 1997).

No Chemical Engineering

So many teachers ask this question: how do I group students? Some have heard from classroom management programs that groups ought to be chemically engineered to include one "low" student, two "medium" students, and one "high" student, seated in a particular pattern so that there is an intentional ability differential between their shoulder partner and their face partner. To that notion, I say, "Hogwash," for three reasons:

First, let's not box students in. When we are asking them to grapple with engaging challenges like building towers of spaghetti or designing a better elbow, who is to say who is "high"? As we know, every one of us has multiple intelligences, and ideally the learning experiences we design for students draw on their full range of abilities.

Second, kids are astute observers and pick up on our beliefs about them as individuals. When we label students and intentionally seat them as such, they are quick to sort out who is who and then as chameleons adapt their behavior: if I look around at my tablemates, knowing every group is comprised of certain ability-leveled roles and realize I am the "low" one in this group, I am likely to lean back and let my peers do the work, to act out the role of "low." This does not suggest a growth mindset on the part of the teacher and does not promote a growth mindset on the part of students.

Third, we all need to learn to get along and collaborate with everyone. When our students get their first job at the Dairy Queen, no manager is going to sit down and plot out who shares each shift based on their GPAs, language backgrounds, and parents' preferences: workers will get assigned hours, and when they show up to work someone is going to have to clean the milkshake maker. They will just need to work it out among themselves. Why not start now?

Our job, as parenting expert Barry Ebert advised, is not to prepare the way for the child, but rather to prepare the child for the way. That is, we support learners best by helping them to develop the resilience and wisdom needed to handle the inevitable bumps in the road, rather than getting out in front of them and working hard to smooth the path. Collaboration is a critical life lesson. Group students randomly. Mix the groups often. This demonstrates to students our high expectations: you can collaborate with any team in this class and succeed. Let yourself be surprised and amazed by what students are capable of doing when we step back and believe.

Special Circumstances

Now, I am going to disagree with myself: there are times when intentional grouping does serve. For English language learners, some engineering can be helpful:

- Students who share a first language can be grouped together in order to explore their thinking in their mother tongue.

- English language learners can benefit from sitting near more proficient English speakers who share their first language and can help, as needed, with translations.

In addition, there are times when homogeneous grouping can support student learning. We might take a few minutes to call together everyone who still needs help understanding negative numbers or the difference between solid, liquid, and gas. Yet I suggest using these sorts of groupings sparingly and fluidly, in order that no one feels pigeonholed or dismissed.

Supporting Participation

Despite our best efforts to randomly assign groups and create accessible tasks inviting multiple intelligences, some students may shy away from participating while others seize the reins. Learners perceived as "low status," either in their own eyes or in the eyes of others, benefit from positive prompting to dive in. We can encourage peers to listen to and respect one another by highlighting the contributions of quieter or less confident learners: visit the group

Voices in the Classroom

"If students choose their partners, they are in better shape. There's more buy-in," explains first-grade teacher Michelle DuMoulin.

"And then I let them know, 'If you are not becoming better mathematicians together, you are going to be apart.'"

When assigning a task, Michelle often invites learners one at a time to get up and to pick their partner. She lets the kids who may be struggling socially pick their own partner first. Each child understands that if he or she is picked as a partner, they can't say no. No one can be unkind.

and invite thinking ("Shaun, what do you think of Dixon's idea?"), restate a child's insight ("So, Celeste is suggesting starting from the top instead of the bottom."), celebrate a unique contribution ("I hear Eve is thinking about this in a brand new way. How would you all respond to her proposal?"). By inserting small comments or queries such as these, then allowing learners to respond, we as adults can use our power to raise the status of overlooked learners, shifting the classroom culture to become more inclusive. Teaching students to listen deeply to one another and to seek the strengths and potential of all supports not only our classroom community but the world at large.

Rituals and Routines

First-grade teacher Carrie Halbasch uses her lunch count every day as a time to practice mathematics: she projects the list of menu options on the board, and as children enter, each adds her own smiley face next to her lunch selection. When the students then gather on the rug, they look at the lunch count together, study the data: Which choice is most popular? What is the difference between the most popular and least popular? How many more people would need to select each choice in order for that option to have ten takers? What other patterns do we notice? These are the kinds of math questions they spend a few minutes on every morning as they begin class.

How might the routines of your day strengthen STEM identities and remind students of their roles as STEM learners in your class? When children know what to expect and what is expected, they can relax and participate fully in each learning experience. Routines and predictability offer students a sense of familiarity and belonging, building their sense of connectedness. Options for rituals and routines abound; let's consider which might serve the purpose of building a STEM community of thinkers.

As Carrie did, consider the ways in which you might add some extra STEM learning opportunities within your regular routine. Here are some ideas and possibilities to add in either daily or weekly as time allows.

- **Counting Circles.** When students gather in a whole group, go around the circle of students and count off by ones, or twos, or fives, or any other number. Talk about what you notice.

- **Number Sequences.** "Take the number of sides in an octagon. Add to it the number of chambers in your heart. Take one third of that. Show me on your fingers what you got." Invite learners to rehearse important concepts and math terms while also rehearsing mental math.

- **Math Games.** "Buzz" was our favorite: instead of saying three, any multiple of three, or any number with three in it, you must say, "buzz." Start at one, each students says a number (or "buzz," as appropriate). Sounds like, "One, two, buzz, four, five, buzz . . ." See how far you can get.

- **Element or Invention or Scientist or Science Demonstration (pick one) of the Day/Week.** You can model this a time or two and then turn it over to students. Let them do the research and the presenting.
- **Puzzler/ Math Mystery of the Week.** Have a STEM challenge alive on the side for students to ponder and discuss. Present it on Monday, let them work on it in their free time, and circle up to discuss on Friday.
- **Current Events.** As described in Chapter 1, bring STEM-related current events into your daily or weekly routine.
- **Ethical Dilemmas.** Many scientific discoveries present ethical challenges; many social problems can be addressed using engineering and technology. Explore some of these issues with students through a moral lens in regularly scheduled discussions.

What other routines might you include in order to elevate STEM thinking on a regular basis?

Your days are full and the weeks fly by, yet with intentional planning and systematic routines, you can fill those five minutes before recess or some slack time after specials with intentional routines that scaffold learners' STEM identities. Once you have decided on which routines you want to implement, take some time to plan ahead—stockpile articles, plan number sequences, or research inventions—these can arm you with months of content at a time. Also, see how you might be able to turn over some aspects of these routines to learners: with support, they can take the lead in planning many of these suggested activities once they have seen you model a few times. Figure 4.2 suggests one possible week's schedule.

Figure 4.2 A Week of STEM Routines

	Monday	**Tuesday**	**Wednesday**	**Thursday**	**Friday**
Morning Meeting	Counting Circle	Counting Circle	Counting Circle	Counting Circle	Counting Circle
Opening STEM work time	Puzzler of the Week (Intro)	Number Sequence	Number Talk	Number Sequence	Puzzler of the Week (Share)
Right after lunch	STEM Current event		STEM Current Event		STEM Ethical Dilemma Discussion
Before dismissal	Element of the Day	Scientist of the Day	Element of the Day	Scientist of the Day	Invention of the Week

Beyond Calendar Math

Many teachers work calendar math into their regular routine as a means to teach the days of the week, months of the year, and other important aspects of how we humans keep time. Consider as well that your calendar math could include interesting instruction about what our calendar really represents: a year is the time it takes the Earth to make one trip around the sun; a month is (approximately) the time it takes for the moon to revolve around the Earth, and a day is the time it takes for the Earth to rotate once on its axis. The seasons are caused by the Earth's tilt, and the phases of the moon are a result of the amount of the sun's light we can see reflected off of it, based on the relative positions of the Sun, Earth, and Moon. Share this with students. Talk about the equinox and the solstice. Ask "Why is the sunset getting earlier? Is the moon waxing or waning? What is an eclipse?" Explore the stories behind the calendar.

Classroom culture is the petri dish in which student thinking flourishes. When we carefully attend to all aspects of the climate—intentional environments, agreements, flexible groupings, and routines, as well as the specific nature of students' learning experiences (as will be discussed in later chapters)—we create fertile ground for learners to grow their STEM thinking as well as their STEM identities. The ultimate test of classroom culture is this: Would *you* like to be a STEM student in your classroom today?

CHAPTER 5

Content: STEM Is Interconnected

Teacher Belief	Teacher Behavior	Learner Experience	Learner Identity
Science can be organized around big ideas.	Provide conceptual frameworks and link topical studies back to big ideas.	Students experience science as a web of related ideas.	I can connect my STEM learning.

Central Question: How can we present STEM holistically?

My very first job in a school was as a garden-based science teacher: it was the best and worst job ever. My school had a two-acre garden (a former parking lot) and 735 kindergarten through 5th grade, mostly bilingual, students. My role was to take every child in the school out for a hands-on science lesson every week. Do the math on that: 735 students divided by five days is 147 kids a day, and if you put them into groups of around twelve (safer group size than thirty when shovels are involved), that's about twelve groups per

Science is built up of facts, as a house is with stones. But a collection of facts is no more a science than a heap of stones is a house.

—Henri Poincare, *Science and Hypothesis*

Stop and Think

- What relationships do you see within the body of STEM knowledge?

- How do you support learners in making connections between new learning and prior knowledge?

day. Subtract lunch, recess, and transition times, and I ended up with an average lesson length of twenty minutes. With no built-in planning time and two languages to consider, I decided we would all study the same thing.

November—earthworms. I got a whole mess of them at the bait and tackle store. We held them, watched them, drew them, labeled them, fed them, and so forth. Then one day midstream in our worm immersion, one little rascal grabbed my leg, "Maestra!" He hollered at me, "Teacher! Why worms?!"

I smiled down at his inquisition, smiled, and admitted to myself: I had no idea. "Don't you love them?" I asked.

His reply: "No."

Next group.

So, why worms? Why anything, when it comes to science? There are so many topics to explore! Each elementary school I visit seems to have a list at every grade level, say, magnets, then weather, then plants, then biomes, then density, then forces and motion alongside fractions and decimals and area and perimeter and integers and probability. A teacher could do a whole lot of activities around each of those, keeping students very happy and busy with hands-on investigations, learning facts and principles about each topic. Is that enough?

What?

What is it about STEM that learners need to know? Understanding STEM means comprehending both the content of the STEM disciplines, as well as these disciplines as ways of thinking and knowing. In Chapter 7, we will explore what it means to think as a mathematician and a scientist and how we can scaffold students' growth along those lines. This chapter is devoted

to examining the content of STEM—what is it that learners do need to know—and how that knowing can be characterized by the qualities of expert knowledge: interconnectedness, understanding, and the ability to transfer (Niemi, Vallone, and Vendlinski 2006).

The Vastness of the Universe

When I was a kid, briefly, I thought my parents knew everything. Now, we have Google, ready to search the Internet's more than 1.2 million terabytes of information with a few keystrokes (Mitchell 2013). I found that statistic on the Web. Information abounds. So, what becomes of our role as teachers in this climate of knowledge overload? No longer are we the purveyors of facts, and no longer do our students need to memorize encyclopedic information by rote. The sheer volume of STEM knowledge captured by humans is exploding as you read these words. Given this reality, we can struggle to decipher what content is important, where to put our focus.

Stop and Think

- What STEM content do you believe is important? Why?

- How do you organize STEM learning to support students in making meaningful connections?

All any of us knows is a tiny sliver of reality. Given this, you can let go of the preconception that you can or need to know everything about STEM before you can teach something. In fact, it can be more fun *not* to know. When we just get curious, think, and learn alongside the students, we have a great opportunity to model grappling.

I have yet to meet a teacher who complained that there were too few standards, not enough kits or projects or resources to fill a school year. The truth is, we all agree: there is just too much. Every teacher I know has a lineup of activities or units she is expected to squeeze in that year, and no one ever seems to feel like there is enough time to do them all justice. When it comes to science, technology, mathematics, and engineering, what is it that is really worth knowing?

Big Ideas

When students study STEM as a long survey of disparate ideas to be memorized and set aside, they come to think of science and math as a disjointed collection of information. With little or no mortar to bind the bricks into a holistic picture, students struggle to make meaning and remember, as well as to believe that science itself is graspable.

According to science education professor Norman Herr, expert knowledge is distinct from novice knowledge in that experts recognize and remember meaningful patterns. "Their knowledge is not simply a list of facts and formulas that are relevant to their domain; instead, their knowledge is organized around core concepts or "big ideas" that guide their thinking about their domains" (Herr 2007). In order to support learners in developing expert knowledge that they understand, retain, and can reapply to novel situations, we can organize our STEM instruction around big ideas that live beyond the distinct units of our instruction. We can take each new topic, say, worms, and connect it to a bigger principle of science that will transfer to other concepts and content, say, life cycles.

While the list of units to be taught at your grade level may well already be assigned to you, how you present that content can support learners in understanding overarching ideas of math and science that pervade all their strands. Whether we are working with earthbound earthworms or the big bang, we serve learners best when we strive to provide them with a conceptual framework to support future studies.

Conceptual Frameworks

STEM professionals spend a lot of time zooming in. There are subspecialties within subspecialties: an internal medicine doctor might become expert in infectious diseases, then within the field of infectious diseases, she can become expert on malaria and its treatment. And yet the study of malaria will apply broader principles known to all doctors, even biologists: cause and effect, systems and homeostasis. These big ideas of science can be found in a great many other STEM topics as well.

Big ideas provide us with conceptual frameworks to which we can attach future learning. Without a superstructure in our brains to hold them up and give them meaning, facts blow away like dry leaves on an autumn afternoon. *How People Learn* (National Research Council, 2000), a synthesis of a broad spectrum of research on how students come to make sense of the world, presents three important premises for us to consider throughout our instruction. In order to learn, we need

- connections with our background knowledge,

- conceptual frameworks, and

- opportunities for metacognition.

For now we are focusing on that second premise, conceptual frameworks. (Chapter 7 will explore background knowledge and metacognition in greater depth.) A conceptual framework is a system of understanding, a great file cabinet in our minds that helps us to sort and connect knowledge in meaningful ways.

A champion chess player, researchers Chase and Simon (1973) found, can memorize the location of four times as many pieces on a chessboard as a novice—given that the arrangement of those pieces on the board is meaningful, as though a game were paused midway. Alternately, a grand master and a beginner remember about the same number of chess pieces on a board where those have been arranged randomly. This to say, when we have a sense of the scope of a topic and how it connects with bigger ideas, and can attach new information within that framework, we increase our ability to remember and improve the likelihood that we can reapply that knowledge in a novel context.

Given the importance of conceptual frameworks, how can we provide our STEM learners a meaningful arrangement of topics, a way to grasp the new content they are learning?

Deciding What Is Worthy

While you may not have control over the units or concepts expected to be studied at your grade level, you do have an opportunity to narrate the importance of each topic and its relationship to others within the STEM fields. By consciously striving to provide learners with conceptual frameworks and to ensure their learning is connected to big, transferable ideas, you can make any topics—even worms—worthy of extensive exploration. Let us consider how to make the "what" matter.

Math That Counts

We can slice and dice bodies of knowledge in so many ways. The National Council of Teachers of Mathematics offers us many lists: Principles for Mathematics Education (equity, curriculum, teaching, learning, assessment, and technology); Content Standards Illuminating the Strands of Mathematics (numbers & operations, algebra, geometry, measurement, data analysis & probability); and Process Standards (problem solving, reasoning & proof, communication, connections, and representation). As well, the Common Core State Standards (CCSS) brought us the Standards for Mathematical Practice (coming in Chapter 6). Our challenge is to "represent mathematics as a coherent and connected enterprise" (NCTM 2000, 17).

I wrestled for many months with each of these lists and many more touted as "Big Ideas" of mathematics, including a wonderful collection of twenty-one authored by Randall Charles (2005). The challenge I found with many of the lists titled "Big Ideas" is that they are actually more of a collections of topics—all important yet not overarching principles that recur throughout the various strands of mathematics.

Patterns, for example, represent a truly big idea in math: we find patterns in the study of all of the Common Core's math strands:

- Numbers and Operations—counting systems all rely on patterns

- Algebra—equations generalize patterns

- Geometry—geometric relationships are predictable

- Measurement—the metric system is based on powers of ten

- Data Analysis and Probability—theoretical probability is a documented pattern

For the purpose of providing learners with a conceptual framework that crosses topical and disciplinary lines, I suggest we look to the Next Generation Science Standards' (NGSS) Crosscutting Concepts, a coherent list of Big Ideas (including patterns!) that can integrate STEM learning.

Crosscutting Concepts

The authors of the Next Generation Science Standards (and the Framework they were built on) were considerably generous in their thinking about all the ways in which we might dissect the content of science—providing us with Performance Expectations (a description of what learners at any certain level ought to know and be able to do with their understanding), Disciplinary Core Ideas (a list of all the important topics of science), Science and Engineering Practices (how one ought to experience science learning), and—most interesting to this discussion—seven Crosscutting Concepts. These seven ideas offer learners the conceptual framework they need in order to build knowledge as budding mathematicians, scientists, engineers, and technology users.

Now I get to say to my little helminthologist (worm scientist) mentioned in the opening of this chapter, "We are studying worms in order to understand . . . um . . . energy and matter." And with that, our exploration of earthworms becomes one of examining their role as decomposers in our ecosystem. Alternately, I could just as well suggest that we study worms to make sense of structure and function, looking closely at the way an earthworm's five hearts and single tube digestive system serve its life purposes. Choose whichever crosscutting concept makes the most sense to you for particular content, but connect worms to a big idea, rather than just studying worms for worms' sake. In this way, we support all learners in connecting new facts to a conceptual framework that not only sustains and supports their understanding and remembering across time, but also builds their sense of science as a comprehensible, manageable body of knowledge.

NGSS Crosscutting Concepts for Science and Engineering

1. Patterns. Observed patterns of forms and events guide organization and classification, and they prompt questions about relationships and the factors that influence them.

2. Cause and effect: Mechanism and explanation. Events have causes, sometimes simple, sometimes multifaceted. A major activity of science is investigating and explaining causal relationships and the mechanisms by which they are mediated. Such mechanisms can then be tested across given contexts and used to predict and explain events in new contexts.

3. Scale, proportion, and quantity. In considering phenomena, it is critical to recognize what is relevant at different measures of size, time, and energy and to recognize how changes in scale, proportion, or quantity affect a system's structure or performance.

4. Systems and system models. Defining the system under study—specifying its boundaries and making explicit a model of that system—provides tools for understanding and testing ideas that are applicable throughout science and engineering.

5. Energy and matter: Flows, cycles, and conservation. Tracking fluxes of energy and matter into, out of, and within systems helps one understand the systems' possibilities and limitations.

6. Structure and function. The way in which an object or living thing is shaped and its substructure determine many of its properties and functions.

7. Stability and change. For natural and built systems alike, conditions of stability and determinants of rates of change or evolution of a system are critical elements of study. (National Research Council 2013)

Weather's Big Idea

I recently had the opportunity to work with a fifth-grade science teacher to design a student learning experience about weather. We started with the NGSS, the disciplinary core idea that students would develop a model to describe the ways the geosphere, biosphere, hydrosphere, and atmosphere interact. In NGSS, the crosscutting concepts matched to the unit were scale, proportion, and quantity, as well as systems and system models. As we explored what she wanted learners to know and be able to do—describe unique weather phenomena such as Catatumbo lightning and frost flowers and describe how the four spheres interacted to create each—we realized that another crosscutting concept would serve this study even better: cause and effect.

We decided to design the learning experience to introduce and refine that concept across time: the essential question—the question introduced at the beginning of the unit, revisited several times throughout, and then again at the close of the learning sequence—was, "Cause and effect: What makes the weather?" Throughout their study, students' responses to this question deepened and were enlivened with rich details and examples.

If you are getting itchy right now, concerned that you are supposed to "do" the weather kit they sent up from the district office and that there is nothing in the kit about Catatumbo lightning, say, I offer you this: you are responsible to the standards and the crosscutting concepts, to make sure that students know and understand those. But in the context of any given lab or unit of study, you get to make your own wise decisions about what you emphasize and how. If another crosscutting concept makes more sense to you than the one proposed, adjust. While standards are set, the concepts are just suggestions of how to attach topics to a larger purpose. Work out what is the best way to make the learning meaningful to your students, and you are on the right track. This may mean dispensing with a few tasks from the kit in order to allow time to grapple with others thoughtfully, or to drive a concept home. As long as this is done with intention to favor depth over breadth and understanding over coverage, I think you are safe to chart your own course through your curriculum.

Another study, say, that of probability, might lend itself to the crosscutting concept of patterns, and our work with experimental probability and statistical probability could be used as an example for students of the ways in which mathematicians organize data to make predictions. Rather than studying probability for probability's sake, we can use that study to get smarter about patterns, and reinforce to learners that the work of mathematicians and scientists is to notice, document, describe, and use those patterns to understand the world.

Not every crosscutting concept is intended to touch every STEM discipline, yet if it makes sense to you and you can find examples to support the relationship, you can freely match your topic of study with the crosscutting concept that makes the most sense. The big idea is that we weave in these concepts regularly and thoughtfully to ensure that students see not only the tree but also the forest, the bigger context of STEM knowledge within which their specific unit of study lives. The Next Generation Science Standards offer us suggestions throughout as to which concepts might be aligned to each disciplinary core idea, yet some teachers choose to make matches all their own. What is important is that learners are connecting discrete facts to big ideas as they grow their STEM understanding.

Making Connections

To ensure that learners develop an understanding of the body of STEM knowledge as an integrated, interconnected whole, as well as gain meaningful comprehension within each unit of study, we can be intentional in how we structure learning. Students need guidance and time to build a web of meaning in their minds, and to connect new STEM knowledge to these crosscutting concepts, our big ideas (Figure 5.1).

Planning Big

When we look at the grade-level standards we need to explore in a given year, the list alone can be daunting. Yet taking time to ask "so what?" invites us to be mindful of the bigger picture. Why are we doing what we are doing? How can this topic or another galvanize students' grasp of a big, important, recurring principle in STEM?

As you begin your planning and consider matching crosscutting concepts to your units of study, consider the following:

- The crosscutting concepts are a buffet of options, not a fixed menu children need to be force fed. You get to select which one(s) you want to delve into. Students will have many more years in school to explore the others.

- Everything is connected to everything. There is no "wrong" crosscutting concept for any given unit of study. If it makes sense to you, you will

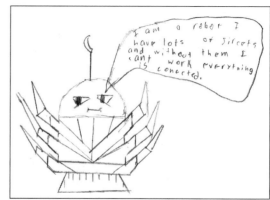

Figure 5.1 Student cartoon: Everything is connected

do a wonderful job explaining the principle in general and the unit of study as an example of it to your students.

- Make meaningful connections. If, during one semester, your class will be exploring endangered species as well as multiplication, why not capitalize on these two topics as examples of cause and effect to bring that big idea to life? But if the connections are forced or flimsy, better to let it go and choose something that truly works.

Figure 5.2 suggests some common topics of study that might connect with each crosscutting concept. I left lots of boxes open to offer you a chance to add your own thinking. What might you add, or move?

Leading with Big Ideas

It's all about purpose: rather than letting learners know that you will be studying geometric shapes because that is the next unit before spring break, why not invite them to explore shapes with you as a way to understand scale, proportion, and quantity, a big idea. Then we can lead with a question: How do mathematicians use scale, proportion, and quantity?

Figure 5.2 Crosscutting Concepts and Topical Examples

	Science	**Technology**	**Engineering**	**Mathematics**
Patterns	Life cycles		Shape strength	
Cause and Effect		Computer programming		Equations
Scale, proportion, and quantity	Solar system		Metric system	
Systems and system models		Design software		Fractions
Energy and matter	Plants		Forces	
Structure and function		Product design		Geometry
Stability and change	Ecosystems		Feedback loops	

You might hand learners protractors and invite them to measure and calculate the sum of the angle measurements for triangles they can find. Then, try out squares and regular hexagons. What predictions can we make about regular pentagons? In this way, the big idea can open a door to learning, inviting a higher perspective on the topic on the table.

One fruitful tool for introducing and enlivening a crosscutting concept is a guiding question. In contrast to topical questions—such as "What is the earthworm's role in our ecosystem?"—guiding questions, as proposed by Wiggins and McTighe (1998), are open-ended and invite broader connections and richer, layered responses. Consider the following as possibilities for bringing each of the NGSS crosscutting concepts to life:

- How do patterns help scientists and mathematicians understand?

- What is the relationship between cause and effect?

- Why is measurement important?

- How do engineers use models?

- How do matter and energy relate to one another?

- What is the relationship between structure and function?

- Why is stability important? Why is change necessary?

You could answer any one of these questions in the context of a given topic. And you can write your own overarching questions as well. They can serve as invitations into an investigation, or as periodic reminders of the context of a study. I encourage you to post your guiding question in the classroom as a visual reminder of what you are all up to, and to take time regularly to circle back and consider it again, layering in your learning.

Patterns and Entomology

When one first-grade teacher's curriculum called for a study of insects, a few weeks on each bug, she dug in and looked for places to zoom out, to get learners curious. She sifted through the science kit, discarded some lessons on insect anatomy, not too concerned that the children memorize the distinguishing number of legs or body segments, and instead chose to think about insects' life cycles as patterns of change.

The day the mealworms arrived in the room, each young scientist (entomologist, as she called them that month) prepared her science notebook with the date and a space to record what she noticed and wondered. Squeals of delight, shouts of joy, and exclamations of excitement filled the air as learners watched their new arrivals very closely on their desks, vigorously discussing leg counts and body shapes and recording their observations in the form of writing and drawing, a routine they would repeat regularly as they observed and documented changes that allowed them to discern patterns in insect life cycles. After each weekly observation of their specimens, their teacher would invite the students to synthesize— "What is changing?" and, later, "What are the patterns?" Across their observations of these and other insects' life cycles, they developed a chart documenting their noticings, the changes they observed. From this data set, they were able to see patterns and generalize about life cycles based on their firsthand experience. Their inquiry into patterns lasted across the year.

All students did come to understand the uniqueness of mealworm anatomy that fall, but not because their teacher told them that was important or expected them to color in a labeled sheet about the body parts. Rather, it was because they were given time to notice, to think, then to think big and make connections to the big idea that life cycles are a pattern.

Keeping Big Ideas Alive

Keeping a crosscutting concept alive throughout a topical unit takes effort and intentionality. Here are some approaches you might try:

- **Reflect:** As you close a new learning experience, invite students to reflect on how their new knowledge builds on their thinking about the crosscutting concept.

- **Document:** Create a place for learners to record how their thinking about a crosscutting concept grows—a notebook, graphic organizer, collection of sticky notes, something they can store and revisit.

- **Expand:** Create time for learners to make connections between the topic of study and other examples of the crosscutting concept at hand. For example, students studying plants through the lens of matter and energy might bring up the topic of their own digestive systems converting matter to energy.

- **Continue to Connect:** Once you have introduced a crosscutting concept within one unit of study, keep it alive in the classroom! Encourage students to find examples of that same concept as they naturally come up in other studies. Celebrate interconnectedness.

Documenting Interconnectedness

My go-to strategy for promoting conceptual understanding amid new learning is the concept map: this open-ended task invites learners to gather key terms or ideas from a study and organize those into a web of meaning for themselves. We might give students the terms or let them develop their own list. Then, the task is to represent those terms—or concepts—visually in a way that illustrates and describes the relationships between them.

Older students can create concept maps on chart paper, writing a word in a bubble, drawing a line to a related term, and explaining on the line how they see the relationship. For younger students, we might provide preprinted words and offer a ball of string as a kinesthetic tool to represent the relationships they see, as in Figure 5.3. More of the explanation could be verbal than written, but the premise is the same: we gain expert knowledge when we take the time to synthesize new learning in a meaningful relationship to that which we already grasp. Try it out.

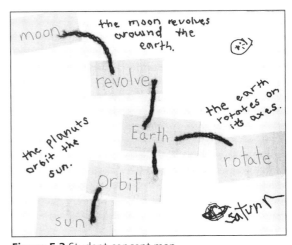

Figure 5.3 Student concept map

When we remain conscious throughout our instruction of the greater web of STEM knowledge, when we remind learners of a conceptual framework that links new ideas with prior knowledge, when we create time for connections and reflection about crosscutting concepts, we invite students to establish the foundation of their own expert knowledge in STEM.

CHAPTER 6

Tasks: Scientists Grapple

Teacher Belief	Teacher Behavior	Learner Experience	Learner Identity
STEM learning addresses content, process, and identity development.	Teachers design tasks that generate students' understanding of the what, how, and who of STEM.	Students learn about STEM as professional scientists learn about STEM.	I can grapple with interesting and important science content.

We have to cease attempting to build "teacher-proof" schools with scripted low-level instruction and instead seek to develop (and retain) perceptive, thinking teachers who challenge students with high-quality, interactive, thoughtful instruction.

—Lisa Delpit, *"Multiplication Is for White People":*
Raising Expectations for Other People's Children

Central Question: How do we design rich challenges that promote STEM understanding and identity?

Aware of the challenges faced by many rural families in developing nations simply to access the water essential for life, Piet Hendrikse and his brother developed a heavy-duty plastic, rollable water container that can easily transport fifty liters at a time, saving women and children, those typically assigned this chore, from the backbreaking work of hauling fifteen liters or less per trip in a jug carried on the hip or head. This innovation has allowed girls, once tasked with the time-consuming responsibility for water bearing, to attend school and thereby to elevate the quality of life for their own children.

The development of this Q Drum—described by some as the "reinvention of the wheel" (www.qdrum.co.za/)– represents an excellent STEM innovation: it involved collaboration and complex thinking to apply the principles of physics to solve a real-world problem. We can look to this example as a model of the sort of STEM problem-solving learners relish.

In this chapter, we consider the construction of rich STEM learning experiences that promote learners' thinking, understanding, and STEM identity development.

Stop and Think

- What is the role of challenge in learning?
- What sorts of problems do you invite students to solve?

What Makes a Task Rich?

We build learners' STEM identities when we scaffold learning experiences that intentionally offer them the opportunity to experience science, technology, engineering, and mathematics as engineers and mathematicians, rather than spectators (as in note takers sitting in silent lecture halls).

Before we get to the nitty-gritty of planning rich tasks, let's think about three related issues:

- What do we mean when we say we want students to build understanding?
- How do we want students to experience the process of STEM learning?
- How can a task boost learners' STEM identities?

Let us look deeply into those three questions.

What: Understanding Content

"Copy—dot—flop." That is how my daughter learned to divide fractions. When I asked her why that worked, she said she did not know, but this was what "they told us to do." Gripped by her description, I grabbed some ice cube trays and beans and yarn and launched my own lesson on what a fraction is, what division means, and why on earth one might want to invert the second fraction and then multiply it by the first in order to divide. By the time my generous speech was complete, she was already finished with her fraction division homework worksheet and looked up long enough to complain, "Mom, I hate your math. It's all about understanding, and that is NOT how we do it."

That was a few years ago now, and since then we have come a long way in understanding one another as mathematicians, my daughter and I. What I have tried to convince her is that when all we learn about problem solving is a procedure, we might be in good shape for quite some time—let's say as long as all the problems on the worksheet are well-behaved versions of one another with nothing unusual like a decimal or a mixed number tossed in. But as soon as the game changes, if we don't know the *why* behind the *what* we have been doing, we are likely to struggle to adjusting accordingly. Death to one's math identity: we got it, we got it, we got it, now we don't get it anymore. At all. Recovery unlikely, too many algorithms memorized, far too little comprehension.

The importance of understanding for later transfer was illustrated by numerous studies, several of which are cited in the useful text *How People Learn* (National Research Council 2000). For example, back in 1959, Max Wertheimer and his colleagues taught different groups of students each one method to finding the area of a parallelogram (remember that slanty rectangle?). The group who learned the rote method memorized the formula: base times height. The understanding method group learned to rearrange the parts of the parallelogram, slicing off a triangle from one end and gluing it on the other to create a rectangle whose area was easy to find. Both groups reportedly succeeded in transferring their area-finding skills to similar-looking tasks. Yet, when the researchers changed the task to something novel—deciding whether one could find the area of a given unique shape—the understanding group was able to transfer their knowledge while the rote group responded with "We haven't had that yet."

What About Knowing Math Facts?

Being able to do quick sums in one's head or to rattle off one's times tables by heart makes life easier. But let's not kid ourselves into thinking that computational facts represent the entire body of knowledge of math: math is much richer, deeper and includes conceptual understanding and creative problem solving. When we compare math learning activities in the United States to those in nations that consistently outperform us on international comparative assessments, we see that American children tend to spend far more time on rote recall as compared with Japan and other nations, who lay a much greater emphasis on conceptual understanding.

Yes, the kids benefit from practicing their facts, yet more important is numeracy, the ability to understand and work with numbers. We support numeracy development by inviting frequent and flexible practice with number talks, dot cards, math games and creative problem solving activities. Skill drills and timed tests, on the other hand, traditional staples aimed at supporting math fact learning, have been found to increase math anxiety rather than scaffold success (Boaler 2015a).

What does it mean to understand? As defined by Wiggins and McTighe in their important work *Understanding by Design* and seen in Figure 6.1, understanding can be described in a variety of ways, and demonstrations of understanding can take myriad forms.

Considering what we want learners to understand and what that understanding might look like, how it could be demonstrated in wonderful and unique ways goes a long way toward informing task design. Another helpful angle to consider is how learners will come to understand the processes or practices they will use.

Figure 6.1 Six Facets of Understanding and Sample Demonstrations of Understanding

facet	definition	example
explanation	Able to describe concepts and their significance in detail.	Can identify cloud types and explain why and how they are different.
interpretation	Able to represent scenarios in a new way (in words or pictures, graphs or tables, physically or numerically).	Can illustrate ½ divided by ⅓ with models and sketches.
application	Able to use what they know in novel situations.	Can propose a strategy to preserve prairie dog habitat along Westerly Creek.
perspective	Able to make connections and understand the context of a situation.	Can describe why some farms are organic and others are not.
empathy	Able to get inside of a situation and understand it from another perspective.	Can explain the evidence for and against the theory that the Earth is flat.
self-knowledge	Notice how style, beliefs and habits of mind affect one's ability to learn.	Can describe his or her own beliefs about evolution and religion.

(The six facets are from Wiggins and McTighe 1998.)

How: The Processes of STEM Learning

The authors of our most recent standards spent time considering not only what learners ought to know, but also how they ought to come to know, providing us with standards of practice for science and engineering as well as mathematics. These practices are not a list of activities teachers should perform in front of students, but rather a collection of experiences we can create for students—parallel to the work experience of STEM professionals—as they build their content knowledge:

Science and Engineering Practices from the Next Generation Science Standards (NGSS)

1. Asking questions (for science) and defining problems (for engineering)

2. Developing and using models

3. Planning and carrying out investigations

4. Analyzing and interpreting data

5. Using mathematics and computational thinking

6. Constructing explanations (for science) and designing solutions (for engineering)

7. Engaging in argument from evidence

8. Obtaining, evaluating, and communicating information (National Research Council 2012)

Standards for Mathematical Practices from the Common Core

1. Make sense of problems and persevere in solving them.

2. Reason abstractly and quantitatively.

3. Construct viable arguments and critique the reasoning of others.

4. Model with mathematics.

5. Use appropriate tools strategically.

6. Attend to precision.

7. Look for and make use of structure.

8. Look for and express regularity in repeated reasoning. (Common Core State Standards Initiative 2010)

Throughout a child's STEM learning experience, it would be wonderful for him to visit each of these practices many times, in different contexts, yet trying to pin down all sixteen at once can be overwhelming.

As we examine these collections of practices side by side, some themes (we might call them meta-practices) emerge:

- problem solving

- reasoning

- modeling

- communicating

These four meta-practices can guide our design of students' learning experiences. "How can I get learners to think like scientists or engineers or mathematicians today?" is the ultimate question we need to ask ourselves as designers of rich STEM tasks.

Hands-On to Minds-On

Hands-on emerged as the battle cry for a generation of science kits and curricula, and boy, do kids love it! Messy Play Doh, sloppy sinking and floating activities, newspaper construction—I can hardly help myself either when these opportunities arise. Who doesn't want to build? I recently visited a fourth-grade classroom where the teacher challenged learners to work in groups of three to construct—using only straws and a limited supply of tape—the tallest tower. Silently. For forty minutes. Kids were pointing and waving and sticking and stuffing, making faces and signaling directions. Everyone was engaged, completely. When the timer went off, their teacher declared a winner, and everyone happily went to recess. I asked her on the playground what the kids would do the next day, meaning about the towers activity. As it turned out, she hadn't planned that they would do anything further with it, yet as we spoke, she disagreed with herself: why miss out on using this activity as a launching pad for a study about shapes and strength and the physics of construction? Students could explore what shapes are strongest and why, and experiment with different ones, revise their vision for their towers and engage in yet another round of competition. In this way, she shifted the fun tower construction task from a mere hands-on activity to a minds-on challenge, drawing learners to think hard about forces and strength.

To make the shift from hands-on to minds-on in any engineering task is a matter of considering not simply what students will be *doing* but, more importantly, what they will be *thinking* while working: what is the science concept or principle you would like learners to explore? What questions will prompt that inquiry? How will they document and share that thinking? Figure 6.2 offers some suggestions.

Who: STEM Inspiration

In addition to generating understanding of both the content and process of STEM, exquisite STEM learning experiences get students excited, elevating their STEM identities. Our finest STEM teaching integrates both education and inspiration.

To adjust one's view of one's self, according to science educator Dr. Brad McLain (2012), is the very nature of inspiration. To that end, he researched the attributes of an inspirational learning experience, one that invites participants to see themselves in a new light. While inspiration can have an ethereal, intangible quality to it, McLain found through his work with science teachers that there are four critical attributes that, together, cause learners to re-orient their ideas about themselves as scientists:

- agency—one's sense of what she is capable of doing
- content confidence—one's ability to understand and manipulate content
- emotional connection—one's excitement about and engagement with ideas
- personal relevance—one's understanding of how a topic matters to her and her life

In our instructional designs, we can leverage these qualities intentionally to create opportunities for learners to develop generative beliefs about themselves or reignite their enthusiasm for STEM learning. Let us explore these attributes more deeply in considering what it would mean to bring inspiration to life in our classrooms (Figure 6.3).

Figure 6.2 Hands-On to Minds-On-Engineering Examples

Typical Hands-on Task (Topic)	Possible Enhancement	
	In order for students to think about . . .	Ask them to . . .
	Content	
Build a container to protect a dropped egg (gravity).	Forces	Diagram the forces acting on their egg.
Build a sling psychrometer from a given kit (weather).	Measurement	Design an instrument that would gather data about _____.
Build a boat that can hold two Lego figures (buoyancy).	Displacement	Think about Archimedes' bathtub and make connections between his work and their own.
	Process	
Build a bridge of newspaper and tape (engineering).	Teamwork	Notice how their group collaborates, where difficulties arise, and what supports them in solving problems.
Build a balloon-powered vehicle.	Design	Record each design they develop, document changes and revisions and explain why those decisions were made.

Figure 6.3 Designing for Inspiration

Attribute	If we want students to believe . . .	We intentionally design experiences so that they . . .
Agency	I am capable.	• Succeed in applying thinking strategies and other tools to solve problems. • Recognize how their own perseverance and growth mindset serve them.
Content Confidence	I know how to do this.	• Acquire new skills and knowledge just in time to apply them to rich tasks. • Know how to access additional resources and information as the need arises.
Emotional Content	I feel excited and want to do this.	• Are drawn in by a reason to care about a problem, idea, or learning experience. • Bring their own creativity and insight to the task.
Personal Relevance	This work is meaningful.	• Understand how their learning connects with their lives outside of school, present or future.

Planning Rich STEM Tasks

A rich STEM task might be a single lesson or a significant project that spans a semester. Regardless, it can illustrate our vision for student learning by generating understanding of (1) STEM knowledge contextualized within a Big Idea; (2) the process of coming to know as a scientist; and (3) one's self as an inspired STEM learner. A tall order! To develop rich tasks, we can either transform existing ones or create new ones all our own.

Creating and Adjusting Tasks

As you look at your current resources, you may have a great many typical tasks available to you, perhaps some you and your students have grown to love. You may need to look no further

for rich opportunities to weave in practices and inspiration. Or, you may want to create tasks from scratch. In either case, I suggest taking a page from Stephen Covey's book, *The 7 Habits of Highly Effective People* (2004), and begin with the end—the content-understanding goals or learning targets—in mind. From there, we can ask ourselves, if a child really knew and understood this topic, what might she be able to do, using the NGSS and Common Core practices, to demonstrate that understanding? And from there, how can I hook her in with a sense of agency and a reason to care? Task design does not always flow in that very order, but this line of thinking can serve as a starting place.

So, for example, as I think about having students build block towers, I might note that the content I want learners to understand is about shape and stability: The shape and stability of structures of natural and designed objects are related to their function(s). To this end, which practice(s) might they employ? I am imagining, rather than learners just designing their tower, building it, and being done, this could be an iterative process, a chance for students to revise their designs, working a lot with NGSS Practice 6 of designing solutions. How can I make that inspirational? As students design, create, and redesign, I think they will build their sense of agency. Further, if they are competing with themselves to build something even taller, this might pique their emotional connection to the content . . . so that is how my thinking is growing as I consider how to take the typical task of tower construction and create a rich STEM experience.

A Science-Centered Example

For another example, let's look back to my weather unit mentioned in Chapter 5. The content goal is that students develop a model to describe the ways the geosphere, biosphere, hydrosphere, and atmosphere interact, and we want students to learn this through the lens of cause and effect. When I think about weather and look at the NGSS and Common Core practices, it seems natural that learners might use modeling to demonstrate their understanding, so I am going to figure out a task that invites them to demonstrate their understanding through modeling. Next, I am thinking about how to hook learners by both connecting their prior knowledge to this new learning and creating a reason for them to care about weather, which, for some, is a pretty—excuse the pun—dry topic. I decide we will start with learners' background knowledge about weather and the water cycle, which I know they studied at length, and then make weather interesting by exploring some unusual phenomena to spark their curiosity, such as volcanic lightning and waterspouts that illustrate interaction among those four spheres. So

I have identified my content target, a practice (or process), and some strategies for making the learning highly engaging—even inspirational. So, my task, I am thinking, will be for small groups to each select a rare weather phenomenon (they get to choose from a given set), study how two or more of the four spheres interact to cause it, and then create a model to demonstrate their understanding of cause and effect in that case. That will be the rich task, modeling rare weather phenomena as a means to understanding the interactions behind the weather they experience every day (Figure 6.4).

Figure 6.4 Rich Task Planning Tool

What will students **understand** about the **content**?

Topic (Disciplinary Core Idea)	
Big Idea (Crosscutting Concept)	

How will students come to understand?

Practices • problem solving • reasoning • modeling • communicating	

How will learners experience **inspiration** and **identity**?

Agency: How does this use my skills and knowledge?	
Content Confidence: How can I succeed?	
Emotional content: Why should I care?	
Personal relevance: How does this connect?	

Kits

Many elementary schools across the nation have made significant investments in science kits. While these ready-made units of study offer accessible hands-on science experiences, we can maximize their efficacy when we are conscientious consumers of these resources. To this end, I encourage you to proceed with caution as you prepare to teach a kit-based unit:

- Get smart about the content. While it may be tempting to "let the kit do the teaching," take it on yourself to be familiar with the central topics of the kit. Know which standards the kit is intending to address and how. Do a little research; check out a couple of children's library books on the topics and become familiar with the vocabulary and concepts. In this way, you can ensure that you proceed purposefully through those unit-learning activities you choose to pursue.

- Maintain fidelity to the learning targets, not necessarily to the road map. Often kits offer more activities and ideas than one can reasonably present to learners in the time allotted, especially if we want to allow time for thinking, rich discussion, and reflection. Oriented to the standards and learning targets of each kit, feel free to pick and choose from the tasks or labs proposed and select those that will most significantly launch learning. You do not need to do everything the kit suggests—but you do need to have good reasons for selecting what you *do* do.

- Make learning experiences minds-on. Some kits come with labs and activities that direct learners to conduct experiments and gather data in prescribed ways, inviting them to work more as lab techs than as scientists. Consider increasing learners' opportunities for thinking by trying the following:

  - present the general topic, then invite learners to ask their own questions and design their own investigations
  - welcome learners to think about what kinds of data they will gather and how
  - ask open-ended questions about what meaning the data offers
  - create time for students to present and discuss their findings, and the similarities and differences between them
  - offer opportunities for learners to revisit their original questions, then to pose and research new inquiries
  - dwell in curiosity and uncertainty

A Math-Centered Example

In seeking to create an inspirational math learning experience for her third graders while also keeping on track to meet state standards for geometry and computation, Ashley Bromstrup created a differentiated project for her class based on the question, "Is the space inside our school shared fairly?"

At her request, her school's principal wrote a letter to the students: the letter described how the growing school would be adding fifth-grade classes in the coming year, and that she wanted to be sure the classrooms the fifth graders were going to use represented an equitable use of space. The third graders decided on their own that they should split into teams, measure each current and future classroom, and hold their data in a table. Teams were dispatched throughout the building to discern the area of each classroom, to learn the number of pupils enrolled in each, and then to share data and develop their own arguments. Each team of students measured three classrooms. Some students took a look at volume, windows, and storage, not just floor space, as they developed their own answers to the open-ended question. Moving beyond area and perimeter, conversations expanded to consider the very nature of justice. Each learner's work culminated with her writing an individual letter to the principal regarding the building's allocation of space. Students enthusiastically dove in.

"This lent itself beautifully to differentiation," Ashley describes. "Some rooms were tiled with one foot squares so they could be easily counted; other rooms were carpeted so students used yardsticks end-to-end to measure. Students who wanted to pursue the idea of volume had support from our gifted teacher as a further extension of the project." Each group drew each

classroom they measured on graph paper and wrote a letter to that class' teacher describing their results. This coming year, Ashley plans to repeat this project and to expand it by asking students to build three-dimensional models of each room they measure.

This task was a far stretch from the area and perimeter work typical math books invite kids to do: look at pages and pages of two-dimensional, labeled drawings and insert the missing areas and perimeters. I completed those worksheets myself in school, and I came out alright, so don't get me wrong, there is no crime in them, but the truth is that they were utterly forgettable. What Ashley's students did reached a level that Dr. McLain would call inspiration: excitement, enthusiasm, learners fully immersed in the belief that not only are they mathematicians but that the work of math itself is utterly loveable, and that their work matters. How did she do that?

Ashley started with the standards. She read them over, knowing ultimately she was accountable to those. Then she asked herself, "So what? Who cares?" and considered how to possibly make the topic itself relevant, interesting, and accessible to eight-year-olds. Ashley's answer came in the form of a strategically designed task that engaged students in meaningful content learning through an open-ended, collaborative process. Based on their readiness and interest, learners explored different rooms in the school, measured them in different ways, and recorded their attributes appropriately—built-in differentiation.

Accessibility

Our classrooms are full of diverse learners with unique strengths and needs, and often we need to differentiate projects to ensure that all are engaged and learning. As you think of revising or redesigning familiar tasks, the responsibility to also differentiate might feel daunting. Yet often this can be easily accomplished when we find the right challenge, one with what Dr. Jo Boaler calls "a low floor and a high ceiling."

Consider the three projects suggested in Figure 6.5:

- Observing and recording animal behavior: Both a kindergartner as well as a world-renowned expert like Jane Goodall can participate at an appropriate level of detail and density.

- Explaining and illustrating the difference between addition and subtraction: Learners at various levels could present a variety of different models at varying levels of complexity as well as work with different numbers, again increasing or decreasing the level of challenge.

Figure 6.5 Rich Task Examples

In order for students to . . .	Instead of asking them to . . .	Try inviting them to . . .
Learn about living things	Label and memorize the parts of a meal worm	Observe meal worms and record their behavior.
Understand basic mathematical operations	Complete a page of one-digit addition and subtraction problems	Explain and illustrate the difference between addition and subtraction.
Appreciate energy flow in a system	Set up a circuit by replicating a diagram	Assemble batteries, wires, and bulbs in as many ways as they can to make light.

- Assembling batteries, wires and bulbs: Challenge level could be increased or decreased by offering fewer or more elements into the circuit as well as adding various requirements for circuit design.
  - These examples illustrate how an open-ended task can be created and facilitated in ways that allow for natural differentiation, far more so than expecting everyone to be doing the exact same thing.

With that, a word of caution: Let us not be the ones to decide which students are or are not ready for a challenge. If we give the Soaring Eagles group access to the microscopes while offering the Bumbling Bluebirds only hand lenses to use, what does that say to anyone about our growth mindset regarding them as scientists? As you differentiate, I encourage you to keep an open mind about who is ready for which level of rigor and to create an environment of challenge by consistently offering student choice. In this way, we can ensure access to rigor.

In order for learners to come to understand not only STEM content but also what it means to be a scientist and to see themselves as such, they need rich learning opportunities that invite them to grapple with rigorous challenges. To this end, we can modify existing tasks while remaining loyal to content standards in order to ensure that all students have the opportunity to grapple with engaging tasks. But when we present steep challenges, learners often need scaffolds and support in order to persevere. These will be discussed in Chapters 7 and 8.

CHAPTER 7

Thinking: Scientists Are Thinkers

Teacher Belief	Teacher Behavior	Learner Experience	Learner Identity
Scientists are thinkers.	Scaffold opportunities for learners to think deeply.	Practice thinking strategies and discourse as tools to support understanding.	I have and can use tools for independent and collaborative problem solving.

Central Question: How can we foster students' independence as mathematicians and scientists?

"On the way to the carpet, talk with a friend about how you might already be monitoring for meaning in your math work," third-grade teacher Caitlin Moore invites. Once students gather, Ms. Moore continues, describing a time when she herself as a mathematician misread some instructions and had to circle back and revise her own work because she had become confused. Ms. Moore relates that experience to their work as mathematicians: the need to monitor for meaning.

> *Children must be taught how to think, not what to think.*
>
> —Margaret Mead

After revisiting the terms *compare*, *estimate*, and *precise*, Caitlin orients students to the day's math challenge by showing some of yesterday's work on the document camera, a word problem that ultimately invited the solver to estimate, then calculate, a distance (87 – 59 km). Today, students will be estimating, then solving another problem. Her invitation to learners: "Pay attention as you work to when you are monitoring for meaning."

"Here is a part where a lot of us are getting stuck: compare your estimate to your precise answer; ask yourself, 'Is my answer reasonable?' If something is reasonable, it's asking, 'Does it make sense?' Harrison put it really well yesterday: 'Does the answer fit the problem?'"

Ms. Moore refers back to their prior work, "Why would it be reasonable to say, '28 makes sense because my estimate was 30'? Why would that make sense?"

"It would make sense because if you took the 87 – 59," a student explains, "You would get close to 30, which was your estimate."

"What would happen if my estimate and my precise answer were super far away from each other?" Ms. Moore inquires.

"Your precise answer might be wrong."

"Or your estimate might be wrong."

"So, if that happens, what should I do?"

"Go back and monitor for meaning. Try solving again."

By offering learners thinking strategies such as monitoring for meaning to support their work as problem solvers, Caitlin arms students with the necessary tools to persevere through rigorous inquiry. As we intentionally apprentice learners as thinkers, we prepare students to engage as mathematicians, scientists, and engineers in the meaningful and complex work of making sense, a life of problem solving.

Stop and Think

- What does it mean to be a STEM thinker?

- In what ways do you intentionally scaffold and promote students' STEM thinking?

Grappling: The Importance of Struggle

As noted by the Tennessee Department of Education,

> *Students often struggle to solve high-level tasks. Their discomfort with the struggle when they are solving the high-level task causes them to ask the teacher for assistance. In turn, the teacher provides assistance, often by doing the problem solving for the student. The students, as a result, do not have the opportunity to learn to think, reason, and to practice engaging in problem solving and communicating.* (2014)

When we see students struggle, we can be tempted to retreat or rescue. Yet when instead we can take care to provide support in ways that do not take the thinking and learning away from students, we facilitate their own process of coming to understand.

First-grade teacher Michelle DuMoulin conducted her own experiment on the value of students' struggle in their learning. She and a humanities teaching partner each share two balanced classes; Michelle teaches math and science to both for half of each day. One year, she chose to directly teach one of the classes how to use in and out boxes in math while she let the other group figure it out themselves. The results were startling: the group that worked it out on their own did amazingly better, understood more, and remembered longer than the kids who received explicit instruction, Michelle reported.

Yet Michelle never just chucks kids into the deep end and expects them to swim unassisted: she intentionally cultivates a classroom culture that is about thinking, sharing, and reflection, a safe place for STEM students to share and grow. She knows that in order to scaffold struggle, she needs to provide learners with tools and then step back and see what they can work out for themselves. To this end, she offers learners intentional scaffolds: thinking strategies and discourse.

Let's look at how we can use these two scaffolds to help our students grapple with ideas.

Thinking Strategies

By inquiring about the ways that successful readers made meaning of text, David Pearson (Pearson and Gallagher 1983) and his colleagues assembled a group of seven distinct but related strategies:

- Using Background Knowledge
- Questioning
- Inferring
- Determining Importance
- Visualizing
- Synthesizing
- Monitoring for Meaning

Soon thereafter, Ellin Oliver Keene and Susan Zimmermann (1997) explored how we might take these effective strategies and explicitly teach them to young students to support their comprehension as readers, with great success. Many wise teachers now share these strategies with learners at all grade levels and across the content areas, offering them as tools for students grappling with new information or problem solving challenges. These thinking strategies may be familiar to you, something you already incorporate into your reading instruction, or perhaps even across the curriculum. Students benefit when we model for them how these thinking strategies they have been using effectively in their literacy blocks or in their lives can also support their STEM learning (Figure 7.1).

Figure 7.1 Thinking strategies

Strategy	General Definition	STEM examples
Using Background Knowledge (Schema)	Making connections between new information and what you already know.	• making connections: math to math, math to world, math to self • applying known facts or patterns to new information
Questioning	Wondering about the content in ways that give me purpose as a thinker.	• asking questions about a problem you are asked to solve • inquiring about phenomena • testing various designs
Inferring	Reading between the lines to draw deeper meaning from a situation.	• deciding which operation or procedure might work best to solve a problem • predicting based on patterns • making decisions about materials or strategies
Determining Importance	Based on your purpose, identifying the main idea and key details.	• finding the question or puzzle to solve • identifying important data • working within constraints to design a solution
Visualizing	Using prior experiences with your senses to relate to the text.	• using manipulatives, drawings, and other representations to show mathematical work • creating models to demonstrate phenomena
Synthesizing	Growing your thinking and understanding over time as you find ways that new ideas connect with content you already know.	• applying knowledge of patterns to make sense of new situations • revising designs in light of test data
Monitoring for Meaning	Remaining conscious of when you do understand, and when your comprehension breaks down; using fix-up strategies as necessary.	• maintaining awareness of when a solution or explanation makes sense • identifying weaknesses or problems in designs or solutions

Voices in the Classroom

First-grade teacher Carrie Halbasch reviews a definition of schema with her students: "what we keep in our memory so we can use it again." Today, she asks learners to explore: "How can I use my schema to help me solve without counting?" They read the problem together aloud:

"7 lions are hunting. 6 hyenas are prowling. How many animals are there?"

After ample independent work time, the group gathers on the rug at the front of the room to share: Devin places his work under the document camera first. "I solved with ten," he begins.

"What schema did you then use as a model to help you prove and double-check?"

"A ten. I drew the first part, seven, then I drew the next part, six. I made it in squares up to ten, and then I had three more. 10 + 3 = 13." He points to the number sentence he wrote under his drawing.

"So, Devin had schema about tens that helped him."

Mia shares next. "What schema did you use?"

"I know my doubles. I know seven and seven makes fourteen, and so six and seven is one less, thirteen."

Ms. Halbasch invites Mia to show how her strategy works and hands her a stack of Unifix cubes. Under the document camera, Mia makes a stick of seven cubes, then another seven. As she is working, Ms. Halbasch coaches the class. "While she is showing us, you can be asking yourself, 'Is this a strategy I can add to my schema?'"

"This is Mia's schema." Her teacher narrates the two matching columns of seven Unifix cubes: 7 + 7 = 14. "Now, Mia, show us what you did."

"I did seven plus seven, then I took away one and it was thirteen." She shows the group by clicking one cube off her model.

"So, your schema about doubles helped you."

Teaching Thinking Strategies to STEM Learners

To teach thinking strategies is to offer learners transferrable tools they can use for the rest of their lives. As in literacy learning, students benefit from explicit modeling of and conversation about how the thinking strategies apply in any given content area. Start by observing your own authentic use of the strategies as related to your STEM thinking and learning. Noticing and naming your own thinking for yourself prepares you to model and explain to your students how you use your thinking to make meaning of STEM challenges.

We use thinking strategies in real life all the time. When I found a leak in my basement last week, I started with my background knowledge: I know that the water in my house runs through pipes and appliances, so I checked around the washing machine, the visible plumbing in the ceiling, and the drain of the sink to see whether there were any detectable leaks. I found none. I asked a question, "Where else could water come from?" That question led me to remember the tap on the outside of the wall, right above the puddle. Sure enough, that had been left on, and was the source of our excess water. My background knowledge and questioning helped me problem-solve. I can tell this story to learners as an example of how I automatically relied on these strategies at home; similarly, as intentional problem solvers, we can all practice the same strategies flexibly.

When we open up our own private thought processes to learners, we invite them in to understand how we ourselves make sense, to see that thinking is a process, not a magical invisible act. By knowing the strategies, seeing examples of their application, practicing them intentionally and reflecting on their efficacy, students can learn to use these tools as independent problem solvers.

We can introduce thinking strategies in a combination of ways:

- Talking about the strategy in the real world, how we all already know and use it, as in, "Just this morning, I made an inference: I looked outside and saw the bright sun and decided to wear my sandals."

- Creating an anchor chart, like a one-frame cartoon, reminding all what the strategy means for STEM learners (see Figure 7.2)

Figure 7.2 Inferring Anchor Chart

Matching a Thinking Strategy to a STEM Learning Experience

Rather than learning and employing all the strategies all at once, students benefit from practicing them one or two at a time. We can support this practice by intentionally providing a process-learning target—a thinking strategy—alongside a content-learning objective for a given unit.

Not every unit of study lends itself to every thinking strategy. While it may be tempting to run one strategy across students' learning, both in the humanities and in STEM, it may not always serve, so take caution and be thoughtful in your decision. Here are some questions you might ask yourself in selecting which thinking strategy to connect with a STEM study:

- What are the main learning activities?

- What kinds of problems will students be solving?

- What sorts of thinking will naturally arise?

- Which strategy most naturally mirrors the work of professional mathematicians or scientists in this field?

Many teachers notice that it can be difficult to tease just one thinking strategy out, since they are so interconnected and interrelated. Nonetheless, students benefit when we notice and name the strategies one at a time, inviting them to intentionally practice a specific strategy in a certain context, while knowing they are inseparable.

- Describing the strategy in the context of our content, as in, "Scientists draw inferences all the time: they look at data and find patterns and use those patterns to make predictions. That is what meteorologists do when they predict the weather."

- Modeling the use of the strategy in our content area, as in, "As I look at this graph we created of the daytime temperatures this week, I notice that for three days in a row, the warmest time of the day was the afternoon. Based on that, I am inferring that this afternoon will be a good time to go outside and test our weather equipment."

- Modeling and scaffolding the practice of the strategy in content-area reading, as in, "I read that 'Meteorologists collect data,' but the article does not tell me how they do that, so I am inferring that they use instruments like the ones we have in our classroom weather station."

- Modeling and scaffolding the practice of the strategy in problem-solving work, as in, "As I look at the thermometer, I notice that only some of the lines are labeled, and between 20 and 30 there are four marks. My background knowledge tells me that science-measuring tools are marked in equal increments, so my inference is that each of those marks is worth two degrees."

- Supporting the use of the strategy with explicit graphic organizers or note-taking formats (see Figure 7.3).

- Inviting learners to reflect on how the strategy helps them to understand and remember, as in, "How many of you found yourselves drawing inferences today? What were they? Do you still agree with yourself? How did the work of inferring support your thinking and understanding?"

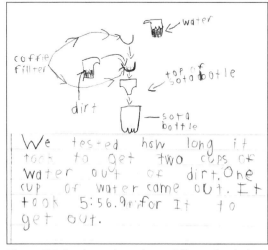

Figure 7.3 Student science journal illustration helps readers visualize his work.

Thinking Strategies and Practices: A Convergence

In the previous chapter, you looked at two lists—the Common Core's Standards for Mathematical Practices and the Next Generation Science Standards—cataloguing sixteen practices in all, and now here are seven thinking strategies. That's twenty-three items, and you are probably wondering, "Am I supposed to do all those?" Not to worry. Whichever of these twenty-three you touch on intentionally and explicitly this year are a gift to your students; they will have many more years in school to experience the rest.

And how do they all relate? They each offer a different lens on the elephant of understanding. We don't need to look at them all at once; we can select what serves learners as we target a specific understanding goal.

In essence, the strategies are like stepping stones toward the experience of the practices. Let us take a look at the themes, or four meta-practices, I proposed and look at the ways in which our thinking strategies might support each (Figure 7.4).

Discourse

Whoever is doing the reading, writing, and talking is doing the thinking. You can buy that statement printed on T-shirts and posters these days. But rather than funding someone else's creative genius on Etsy, the best advertisement for this principle is to bring it to life in your own classroom: let the kids do the work of problem solving.

Thinking Strategies for Classroom Management

"When I look over here, what do you think I am inferring?" a teacher asked her first graders during paired work time.

"That we are not working," a child replied. His teacher smiled and moved on.

"What are you determining is important right now?" a teacher asked a youngster grinding away at the pencil sharpener during independent math time.

Thinking strategies can be kept alive throughout our days not only as tools for learning content but also as lenses through which we can invite students to reflect on their behavior. How else might you use a thinking strategy reminder to draw forth the best from a young scientist?

Figure 7.4 Thinking Strategies Support STEM Practices

If we want learners to . . . (Practice)	We might provide explicit instruction on how to . . . (Thinking Strategy)	Learners might ask themselves . . .
Problem Solve	• Use Background Knowledge • Monitor for Meaning	• What do I already know about this? • What would make sense?
Reason	• Ask Questions • Infer	• Why? • What do I predict?
Model	• Visualize and Represent	• How can I show what I understand?
Communicate	• Determine Importance • Synthesize	• What is important to share? • How did I figure this out? • Why does this matter?

Building Community by Responding to the Thinking of Others

In addition to supporting students in responding to peers' ideas and questions respectfully in the context of whole-group and small-group discourse, fourth-grade teacher Jeff Lewis also creates a space for students to blog about—and respond to peers' blogs about—their thinking and learning as scientists and mathematicians. This online forum serves as a wonderful space to expand their community of learners to include parents and friends. The opportunities provided by technology invite us to expand learners' audience while also teaching about how members of a learning community exchange ideas and respond to the thinking of others.

As we offer learners steep challenges and thinking strategies to access them, peer conversation becomes critical to their success. As education researcher Lev Vygotsky (1978) described, students can meet more stringent challenges collaboratively than alone, so if we do pitch their work in what he calls their Zone of Proximal Development, they will need social support in order to persevere and succeed. Discourse is a crucial ingredient to success for scientists of all ages—that is why STEM professionals hold conferences all over the world, meet in online chats, and discuss their thinking in numerous forums. As humans, we need each other to ignite and push our thinking.

Chapter 4 describes a classroom culture that creates a fertile climate for generative discourse. With those norms and expectations in place, we can invite learners to engage with peers in both small- and large-scale conversations about their understanding.

Language acquisition researcher Jeff Zweirs explains the importance of discourse for learners, "The better students get at negotiating and explaining content ideas, the better they learn them. The better students get at communication, the better prepared they are for communicating in college, careers, and life" (Zweirs, O'Hara, and Pritchard 2014). Discourse in pairs, small groups and with the whole class all contribute to learners' thinking and language development. For all students, but for English language learners in particular, small opportunities for oral rehearsal articulating their thinking can prime the pump of their ideas and increase their capacity and courage to both share before the whole class and demonstrate their ideas in writing. For these reasons, discourse is a critical scaffold to student thinking and understanding.

The purpose of discourse is to create an intentional time, place, and audience for students to share and grow their thinking. Here are some concrete steps toward that purpose.

Structures for Discourse

Discourse can certainly take place among the whole class as a group, and yet more voices can be heard when we invite students to talk among themselves. Some structures for whole-group sharing and discussion will be presented in Chapter 8.

Here let us consider how to get small groups of learners talking. You probably have a fistful of ideas already, but here are a few principles and suggestions.

- Keep groups small. The fewer of us there are, the more we each get to say. Pairs can be sufficient, but for juicy topics, try trios to introduce a wider range of opinions and ideas (Figure 7.5).

- Keep the time tight. Conversation will expand to fill whatever time is allotted; having some (but not too much) time pressure sustains learners' motivation to efficiently share.

- Give specific directions. The vague instruction to "talk about your thinking" does not provide learners with as much support for success as "describe the changes you made between your first model and your second model and why." Be clear about exactly what you expect. Sometimes sentence stems can be a useful scaffold to this end.

- Mix groups often. I am a big fan of random grouping. Invite students to pair up by shirt color, shoe size, number of siblings, birth month . . . anything. Or let your electronic tools create the groups. Either way, mixing often reinforces the reality that we all need to collaborate in a collegial community of learners and that there is no one we can't talk to.

- Rehearse and use familiar structures. Gathering in pairs or trios might be the only discourse format you use, but learners still need to practice and learn the norms of these structures, and to reflect on their own adherence to them.

Figure 7.5 Thinking-Strategy Prompts for Paired or Small-Group Discourse

Thinking Strategy	Invite learners to talk about
Using Background Knowledge	• What helped you get started? • How did this connect to what you already knew?
Questioning	• What did you wonder about? • What questions did you ask yourself? • What do you still want to know?
Inferring	• What were you inferring? • How did inferring help you?
Determining Importance	• What's the most important thing you figured out? • What do you want to remember?
Visualizing	• What models helped you understand? • What models could you create to show your understanding?
Synthesizing	• What does this connect with? • How does this relate to the Big Idea? • What are you learning about yourself as a scientist or a mathematician?
Monitoring for Meaning	• How do you know for sure? • Why does it make sense?

Discourse Norms: TACT

You may already have your own set, but here's a little acronym to try with your students: TACT, for Turns, Attention, Curiosity, and Thanks.

- *Turns.* Share the airtime.
- *Attention.* Listen with your whole body; when speaking, focus on your audience.
- *Curiosity.* Inquire of the sharer to deepen your understanding.
- *Thanks.* Appreciate your partner by offering gratitude and specific feedback.

Respectfully Disagree

Disagreement is inevitable; students need productive ways to express their disagreements. Teach students to critique peers' ideas, not to attack individuals personally. We can model statements requesting clarification rather than triggering argument:

- Could you help me understand why you . . .?
- I'm not sure about the evidence used . . .
- How are you connecting that?

When learners really listen to peers' thinking, they can effectively tease out classmates' misconceptions and, with practice, gently offer feedback that supports collective understanding.

Accountability for Discourse

"What if they just talk about the World Series?" one teacher asked me as we discussed how she might introduce more discourse into her students' learning experiences. That is indeed the fear: what if time to talk about thinking becomes time wasted? We need to hold students accountable for discussing what we've just asked them to explore and can do so in a number of ways, changing frequently, after a discourse opportunity. Consider the following:

- **Independent application:** invite learners to work alone to use what they just discussed: solve a problem, sketch a diagram, and so forth, to document their understanding.
- **Writing:** ask students to record what they learned or are thinking now in their notebooks or on an exit ticket to be handed in.
- **Warm calling:** after offering learners time to warm up by thinking, writing, or speaking in a small group, randomly call on one or more students to report the content of their small-group conversation.

These quick demonstrations of accountability may take a few tries to sink in, and learners can be supported in using their discourse time wisely when reminded beforehand, "This is a chance to share your thinking and to hear the thinking of a classmate. You will need that thinking, so please make a good choice about how to use this time."

Time for Discourse

Life is so busy that it is tough for all of us to take the time to stop and think, to talk, and to listen. And yet, that is when the learning happens, when we are challenged to articulate our thinking and then reflect on it in light of the thinking of others. Discourse presses us to synthesize and to own our ideas. Invite learners into this intellectual exercise often and much—we need not save it until the end of a lesson or a task. Sometimes quick discourse creates just the momentum needed for learners to persevere.

You are a problem solver. This is the most important message we can offer learners about themselves. Thinking strategies serve as tools to support problem-solving success, and discourse creates a time and a place to flex our thinking muscles.

When we take the time to intentionally explain, model, scaffold, record, practice, and reflect on how these thinking strategies serve our STEM understandings, we support learners in internalizing these tools for their own future independent use.

CHAPTER 8

Workshop: Understanding Takes Time

Teacher Belief	Teacher Behavior	Learner Experience	Learner Identity
In order to learn, students need to work hard.	Create and facilitate workshop model lessons.	With support, students spend the majority of their learning time engaged in authentic work.	Students know that they are the architects of their own understanding.

All I am saying . . . can be summed up in two words: Trust Children. Nothing could be more simple, or more difficult. Difficult because to trust children we must first learn to trust ourselves, and most of us were taught as children that we could not be trusted.

— John Holt, *How Children Learn*

"What are some animal adaptations you guys learned about?" Kate Klaver asks her third-grade scientists, all gathered on the rug in front of a screen displaying pictures of uniquely adapted animals from diverse biomes.

"Why do some animals have adaptations? What are they for?"

"Survival," the students agree.

Kate invites learners to share some examples, then calls on hands:

"A three-banded armadillo can roll into a full ball for protection and survival."

"A camel stores water in his humps so he could last a long time without water."

"A spiny lizard gets water in his scales, and then it goes to his mouth. He gets water out of the air because he lives in a desert."

"Great examples of animal adaptations!" Kate affirms. "Do plants have adaptations for survival?" She invites the class to vote, yes or no, in response to this question. All vote yes.

"Today we will talk about seed dispersal, which helps plants survive. What do you think dispersal means?"

"Spreading?" a student volunteers.

"Right, seeds spread out. Why do they do that?"

"If they are dropped right underneath a plant, it would be tough to grow."

"There is competition for sunlight and water."

The class agrees that seeds need to move and gives more good reasons as to why. Then Kate asks them how: how do seeds move? They develop a list of ideas:

- animals—bees pollinate

- wind

- poop

- water

- explosions

Kate added that last one as a tease and uses it to introduce a very short video on seed dispersal. The biologist in the film announces in closing, "Those plants know what they are doing."

"What does he mean, 'Those plants know what they are doing'? Turn and talk to someone next to you." Students go knee-to-knee and dive into discussion of the film, then come back as a whole group and share out.

Kate refers students to their lab sheet, a handout distributed earlier, and engages the group in some shared reading of the learning targets. She annotates her own copy of the sheet under the document camera as they go over the key questions: "How do variations in seeds provide advantages for survival? Which seed characteristics are suited to each method of seed dispersal?"

After quickly introducing the task, Kate offers students time to think, talk, and write on their graphic organizer the qualities of seeds that might be best transported by various means: water, animals, explosion, and so forth. After this investment of time priming the pump of learners' thinking, Kate launches the lab: In small groups, learners will be studying seed specimens, discussing and deciding which dispersal method is most likely for each.

Students don protective gear and move to their table groups of four. Each student carries her science notebook, which contains the lab instructions and recording sheet. Table captains go to the supply cart and select a specimen to bring back to their group for analysis. With hand lenses and careful handling, students discuss each seed, drawing them, writing about them, and making predictions about each seed's strategy for dispersal; then the table captain returns the specimen and brings the group another seed.

For twenty minutes, learners work in their table groups while Kate visits and confers, probing understanding. "What are you thinking? Why?"

As work time winds down, Kate hands each table a card with a dispersal method on it—water, wind, and so forth. She asks each table group to select a favorite seed specimen that uses that method, clarify their claim about its dispersal method, and prepare to present that back to the class. Their claim is to begin with the sentence stem, "This seed has an advantage for survival . . . ."

"Decide on the seed and talk about the evidence. Which of your seeds are you most passionate about?"

Kate talks through her own example, offering her claim, evidence, and reasoning as a model for what she expects learners to present. Then, before shifting to work time, she invites, "What questions do you have?"

After briefly planning their presentations and nominating their spokespeople, groups clean up their lab work and return to the classroom meeting area.

Sapphire places her seed under the document camera and explains, "This chia seed has an advantage for survival because it is small and lightweight and able to float on the water, so it can spread to where it wants to."

The class applauds.

Kate records what Sapphire said, modeling her own writing, "This chia seed has an advantage for survival.

I know this is true because it is able to spread with water dispersal. Our evidence for this is that it is small, lightweight, and able to float." Learners copy.

Alexis shows a seed pod dispersed by water. Evidence: it floats, but the seeds sank. Applause. Addie presents a sunflower seed on behalf of the animal scat dispersal group, and the hitchhiker group presents a sticky burr. Oscar, representing the last group, presents a large seed pod and describes its dispersal by explosion.

"What do you think is the primary method of seed dispersal?" Kate invites learners to consider this question. Animal scat gets the most votes. In preparation for their upcoming field trip to a protected wilderness area—Long Canyon, near Boulder—that is suffering an invasion by myrtle spurge plants, Kate describes the ways in which conservationists are striving to protect the area by having visitors wipe their shoes.

"What is our big takeaway from today?" Kate closes out the lesson. "Why do plants have adaptations?

The class responds with enthusiasm in one voice, "SURVIVAL!"

Kate's class is an exemplary forum for student thinking. She consistently accesses or builds learners' background knowledge, purposefully preparing them to think like scientists about engaging tasks and important ideas, then to record and share their thinking. She folds students' science-learning experiences into meaningful science workshops that ensure opportunities for students to make connections between new learning and prior knowledge as well as to reflect and make meaning.

Physicist Carl Wieman explains, "If you have classes where students get to think like scientists, discuss topics with each other and get frequent, targeted feedback, they do better" (Dreifus 2013). Chapter 6 explored the nature of such tasks; Chapter 7 described the thinking surrounding those. In this chapter, we will examine how all the aspects of STEM teaching and STEM identity development presented so far in this text can be woven together within a day's STEM workshop.

STEM Workshop

Workshop model instruction was inaugurated decades ago by Donald Graves (1983). Graves' vision when he initially crafted the workshop model of instruction for writing hearkened back to the Middle Ages and the apprenticeship model of learning: we as adults, he posed, are the master craftspeople, and our students are apprentices; some of students' learning time, therefore, ought to be devoted to their observing master works—mentor texts, high-quality work samples, exemplary thinking processes—yet the majority of time ought to be devoted to learners enacting similar intellectual feats.

Workshop is a mainstay in many literacy learning environments: teachers launch class with minilessons designed to offer a morsel of just-right instruction on reading or writing in order to support learners' efficient use of independent or shared work time. The bulk of learning time is devoted to scaffolded independent work, perhaps punctuated by a few "catch and release" moments, where the teacher calls for the group's attention to provide additional necessary instruction or direction. As students work, the teacher confers and observes. Typically, a literacy workshop concludes with sharing and reflection, opportunities for learners to come together and show what they accomplished, share what they understand, and engage in metacognition about how the experience was meaningful to them, what they learned about their strategies, and how they grew their identity as literate individuals.

A STEM workshop can be structured very similarly: knowing the rich task we want learners to enjoy during work time, we can use the minilesson to target content learning, process, or strategy instruction, as well as some procedural guidance as needed. During work time, students engage in the work of scientists, prodded by their peers and our good questions, recording their learning as they proceed. Workshops close with opportunities to share work and thinking, as did Kate's students. Workshop is simply a format for instruction and can be used flexibly in response to students' needs, your learning targets, and conditions of time and space. Figure 8.1 offers a visual representation of how time is typically allocated within a workshop.

Some instructional designers these days characterize the format I just described as workshop 1.0 and posit that this is a useful structure for introducing new content but offer another version, workshop 2.0, in which students are invited to grapple with a challenge independently first, at the opening of learning time, before any explicit instruction or guided discussion. This can definitely be a useful format, creating a need to know or a space to apply known concepts before a group lesson. Rather than split hairs over which version of workshop one might employ, I encourage you to stay true to the underlying purpose: organize learning time in order for students to do the hard work of thinking, analyzing, problem solving, and reflecting. Our role as teachers is to facilitate.

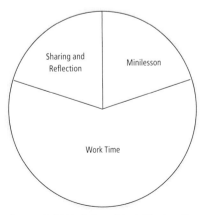

Figure 8.1 Workshop Model Instruction

Planning a Workshop

As you read the description of Kate's lesson, you could see that she did a lot of work in advance to prepare for that workshop: she clarified a rich task, selected photos, chose a (very short) video, designed a lab sheet and graphic organizer, gathered specimens, prepared the lab, and determined an appropriate closing activity. The success of her workshop was built not only on that day's planning but also on the community of learners and structures in place to support their positive participation: agreements and expectations, group work skills, science notebooking experience, and everything students know about what it means to be a science learner. Workshops take work to build. Knowing you built the foundation for workshop based on the previous chapters in this book, let's take the planning of a single day's lesson one step at a time.

Begin with the End in Mind

Start your workshop plan with a clear picture of all the aspects discussed in earlier chapters:

- What is the content learning target?

- What are the practices or process learning targets?

- What is the Big Idea?

- What is the rich task?

Knowing these foundational pieces, you can design each aspect of the workshop to serve your purposes.

Minilesson

In Kate's class, we saw how she used the minilesson time in order to activate learners' prior knowledge, interest them in the task, and warm them up to the sort of thinking about seed form and function that they would later be asked to do independently. Knowing which rich task students will engage with and how, consider what it is learners will need in order to be successful. Based on this, you can design a minilesson that offers appropriate modeling and explanation without taking the work of thinking away from learners.

Here are some key questions to ask yourself when planning a minilesson:

- How will I engage learners' interest; what hook or query will support inspiration, as described in Chapter 6?

- How will I communicate purpose (learning targets)?

- What background knowledge will students need, and how will I invite them to access that?

- What additional background knowledge will I need to build?

- What sorts of thinking will I model and prime?

- What critical instructions about the task do I need to deliver orally?

The minilesson is called such because it is intended to be brief. I myself am guilty of teaching many a maxilesson. Yet according to neuroscientist and *Brain Rules* author John Medina, "it takes you about ten minutes to lose an audience" (Medina 2015). So, let's keep our minilessons below that time limit.

Does Workshop Mean Stations?

No.

Workshop means intentional, scaffolded time for learners to work and think as scientists and mathematicians. Workshop means having a clear purpose, a shared learning target, and meaningful work that students can engage with individually and collectively in order to enhance understanding. Workshop includes sharing and reflection to support metacognition and memory.

If during your workshop work time, you want to have students working in different areas of the room on very different tasks, that can serve, but if those tasks are not targeting a common learning goal, that creates limits to how a collective minilesson or whole group sharing time might enhance learners' understanding.

Work Time

While you already have selected or designed the rich task, consider when planning for work time how you will best facilitate learners' engagement with that task. While many STEM projects or activities invite collaboration, solo think time is a critical ingredient to participation: consider offering students a few minutes to ponder alone before joining their partners; in this way, they will have a higher likelihood of arriving at work with some ideas of their own, feeding the collective insight of their team. During work time, take advantage of your opportunity to listen in, confer (discussed further in Chapter 9) and celebrate learners' thinking. If you can stay out of the roles of police officer, accountant, or administrative assistant and instead play thinking coach, your students will be the better for it.

As you plan for work time around a task, consider the following:

- What is the most appropriate group size for this task? (Base this on the complexity of the task and the opportunities for true collaboration it invites, not on availability of equipment or arrangement of furniture.) I encourage you to limit group size to three except for the most complex projects.

- What could be some stumbling blocks students might face in this challenge, and how will I scaffold their independent problem solving? (Critical: Do the task yourself first. Whether students are going to be building paper bridges or spinning spaghetti sticks, get the same materials they will be using, work within the same time limit you are allotting them, and run the whole task from start to finish. This will illuminate for you how they may get stuck, as well as what else they might need to succeed.)

- What will I be watching and listening for as evidence of student understanding? What questions will I ask learners to prompt their thinking? (See Chapter 7 for ideas.)

- How will learners document their thinking before, during, and/or after engaging with the task?

In addition, it will be helpful to consider efficiency of how materials will be managed, distributed, and cleaned up.

Sharing and Reflection

Tempting as it may be to allow students to build or observe or debate right up to the bell, research on the value of reflection suggests the importance of allowing ample opportunities for learners to share and reflect before wrapping up a learning experience. Helping learners zoom out to the *why* of what they were doing during learning time invites metacognition and supports memory. Planning for sharing and reflection, you might ask yourself these questions:

- In what ways will learners share about the content?
- How will students reflect on the practices or processes they used?
- What conversations will we have about how the experience impacted their STEM identities?

Sharing orally engages learners as a community in explaining their thinking and responding to the ideas of others. If facilitating a whole-group sharing discussion, see the recommendations that follow on facilitating accountable talk.

Reflection can take place in a range of formats: written, oral, or silent pondering. If you go with written, have a plan for how you will gather learners' documentation and use it to drive next steps. If reflection is oral, consider inviting learners to share in pairs or trios, rather than holding the whole group hostage while one or two students describe their experience. Mix up the format and the questions but remain vigilant to the value of this often-missed step in our lesson plans: save time for reflection (Figure 8.2).

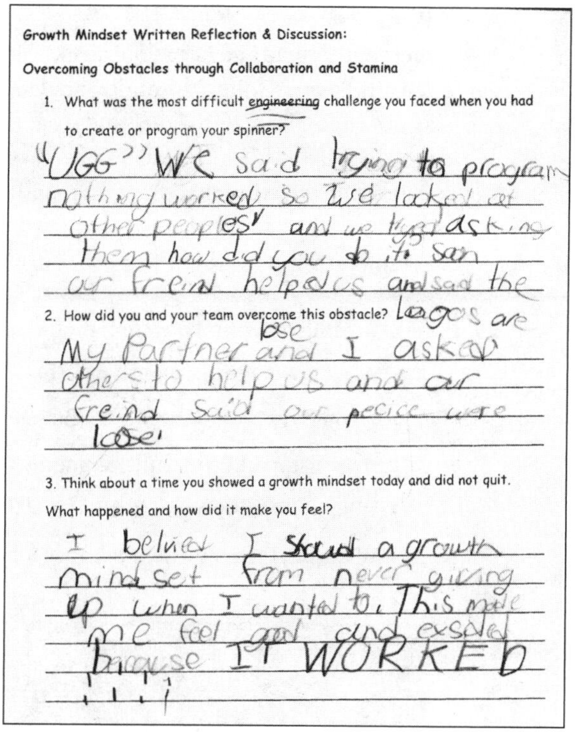

Growth Mindset Written Reflection & Discussion:

Overcoming Obstacles through Collaboration and Stamina

1. What was the most difficult ~~engineering~~ challenge you faced when you had to create or program your spinner?

"UGG" We said trying to program nothing worked so we looked at other peoples and we kept asking them how did you do it? Sam our freind helped us and said the Legos are lose

2. How did you and your team overcome this obstacle?

My Partner and I asked others to help us and our freind said our pecice were lose!

3. Think about a time you showed a growth mindset today and did not quit. What happened and how did it make you feel?

I belived I showed a growth mindset from never giving up when I wanted to. This made me feel good and exsited because IT WORKED !!!!

Figure 8.2 Student reflection

Facilitating a Workshop

My recent book, *Minds on Mathematics* (2012), details each segment of workshop model instruction in the context of middle grades math. Here are some key ideas from the book as they relate to STEM in the early years, although I encourage you to read (and translate to your grade level and content as needed) the whole book if you are interested in further information about workshops.

With so much planning behind them, many teachers come to find that a workshop can run itself—well, kind of. Following are some points to remember to ensure our STEM students keep their focus.

Minilesson

Bring the learners in close, then, as described earlier, be quick, concise, and clear. Hook everyone. Ensure accountability for listening and understanding what lies ahead by checking for understanding before turning students loose for work time.

Work Time

Bite your tongue and keep your distance. Really, you said everything you needed to say in the minilesson. Your class understands your agreements and norms for collaboration. They know where the materials are and what they are supposed to do. Let them work it out. If you rush in too quickly to rescue or assist, you will short-circuit their autonomy and plant in their minds the idea that they can remain dependent upon you. That is death to workshop. Instead, hang back. Prompt with questioning, as needed. If a group is truly stuck, try these common therapy probes:

- What do scientists do when they are stuck?

- What do you think makes sense?

- If you did know, what might you say?

- How else could you think about it?

- What do you wish you knew? How could you find that out?

- What might you do next to move forward?

A common pitfall of collaborative work is dysfunctional groups. As described in Chapter 4, cooperative learning teaches a key life skill. To this end, how can you ensure maximally successful group work that deepens rather than detracts from STEM learning? In my own classroom, I decided one year to go ahead and start the year by brainstorming all the problems of collaborative learning: someone takes over, someone bows out, someone loses the materials, and so forth. I just listened and charted while students recounted all their prior group learning experiences. Then, we handed each problem to a team of learners, and their task was to create a poster of strategies on what to do if, say, someone on your team was being bossy and taking over the project. We hung the strategy posters on the wall, and for the rest of the year, we had a go-to resource (other than me) offering advice to flailing collaborators.

As learners work independently, it can be tempting to dive in to your email in-box or tweet the world about how well your students are working, yet I encourage you to stay engaged with the class. Show interest and enthusiasm and promote effective learning behavior by

- celebrating growth mindsets (described in Chapter 3), as in, "By trying a different way after your first method didn't work, you are showing perseverance";

- noticing and naming successful strategies, as in, "Ethan has decided to sketch out his entire plan before getting the materials"; and

- restating the thinking of low-status group members, as in, "Hmm, so Alexandra is suggesting you start building from the top down." (While I would discourage us from using our power to affirm certain children's ideas over others, I have seen the strategy of shining a light on a particular child's thinking to be effective in elevating peer awareness of the insight of a child they might typically overlook.)

In addition to offering this responsive feedback on learners' behaviors, you might also see patterns of confusion or need in the room. As these arise, decide whether students are in a zone of productive struggle or beginning to experience frustration and failure. If the latter is true, consider quickly calling the group together for some additional instruction or recalibration. In her book, *That Workshop Book* (2007), Samantha Bennett refers to these moments as "Catch and Release," because we catch learners' attention, offer them some input, and then release them back to work.

Sharing and Reflection

Get learners talking. When students explain their thinking and reasoning, they see gaps in their current knowledge and benefit from opportunities to connect new learning with their existing understandings (Chi et al. 1994). Peer feedback is important because it invites students to reflect on their own thinking and respond to the thinking of others, taking teachers out of the role of "verifier of accuracy."

The accountable talk framework provides a useful set of guidelines for promoting effective classroom discussions (Michaels, O'Connor, and Resnick 2008). Accountable talk is based on two guiding principles:

- all students must have access to the learning conversation, and
- the content of discussions consistently furthers understanding.

This means that talk must be accountable to the learning community (providing access to all learners) and accountable to disciplinary norms and knowledge (using STEM reasoning to further STEM understanding). Accountability to the learning community means that students listen to, respond to, and build on each other's ideas. Discussions are exchanges between students, not just students and the teacher. Here are four options in support of accountable talk:

- Ensure that all students can hear one another. Ask, "Was everyone able to hear that?" Students have a tendency to talk directly to the teacher, so a teacher needs to establish the norm that students are talking to the entire class by inviting the speaker to face the group and to use appropriate volume. If you are standing, you can also head to the opposite side of the room from the speaker, indirectly requiring her to elevate her volume and address the whole group.

- Keep everyone together. Ask, "Who can repeat . . . ?" or "How might you say that in your own words?" In addition to hearing one another, students need to understand peers' contributions. We can invite students to re-voice what peers say, as well as ask learners questions to check for comprehension.

- Link learners' comments. Invite, "Who wants to add on?" This helps students respond to one another, rather than just their teacher. When students acknowledge peers' contributions, the contributors feel greater ownership and agency over their ideas, ultimately increasing their investment.

- Verify and clarify. Ask, "So, are you saying . . . ?" Model for students that they can clarify peers' reasoning by paraphrasing, and also that each learner has an obligation to make sure everyone can understand what they are saying.

In addition to following these suggestions to ensure all learners are participating and understood, we can promote thinking in the following ways:

- Press for accuracy. Ask, "How do you know?" or "Is this complete?" Challenge students to provide sufficient evidence from reliable sources.

- Build on prior knowledge. Ask, "How does this connect?" Remind students of relevant prior experiences and knowledge.

- Press for reasoning. Ask, "Why do you think that?" or "How do you know that?"

- Expand student reasoning. Invite, "Take your time; say more."

Wait Time

Deep thinking takes time. Yet most class discussions take place at lightning speed, leaving all but the fastest learners behind. By using at least three to five seconds of "wait time" after posing questions, calling on students, or student responses, teachers can give learners adequate time to think. When students have time to process and reflect on one another's thinking, they are likely to contribute more substantively to the discussion by offering more detailed replies, answering in complete sentences, and connecting their comments to other classmates (Rowe 1986).

These moves can be useful when facilitating a discussion about content, process, identity, or reflection in service of STEM understanding.

With a carefully designed task and thoughtfully crafted workshop, learners can engage deeply in a STEM learning experience that facilitates their knowledge and identity development within a supportive community of learners (Figure 8.3). This chapter offers a lot of instructions and suggestions to that end, yet I encourage you also to lean on what you know and to make the structure of your STEM workshop your own. There are no workshop police. If your students are thinking and understanding as mathematicians and scientists, you are doing this right!

Workshop Planner

Goals: What will students come to understand about content? Process? Big Ideas? Identity?

Task: What learning activity will leverage that understanding?

Minilesson *How will learners be engaged and prepared?*	
Work Time *How will learners collaborate? How will they document their thinking?*	
Sharing and Reflection *How will learners share their understanding and reflect on the learning experience?*	

Figure 8.3

CHAPTER 9

Assessment: Scientists Share

Teacher Belief	Teacher Behavior	Learner Experience	Learner Identity
Students can grasp and retain important STEM ideas.	Teachers communicate learning targets and invite learners to synthesize and share their understandings.	Students know the purpose behind their work and monitor their own progress toward understanding.	I know.

Central Question: How do we invite learners to document and reflect on their understanding?

Shannon Umberger's second-grade students sit in a huddle on the rug in front of her whiteboard. It is time for sharing, and they are working on $100 + 100 + 1000 =$ _____. Two students, side by side, have written their work for the class to examine (Figure 9.1).

Knowing a deep thing well, which is what science asks of its practitioners, is an empowerment that is very profound. It's a liberation.

—Ann Druyan

"Find a partner," Shannon invites. "Talk about whether you agree with the way Marin did it or the way Luke did it."

After a few moments of partner talk, the group comes back together to share their thinking. "Did you all agree with your partners?" Shannon inquired. Many nods and hands raised. "How many of you agreed with Marin's work?" A few hands reach for the ceiling. "And who agreed with Luke's?" More hands. "Who can explain?"

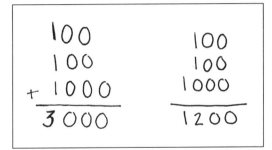

Figure 9.1 Student work on the whiteboard

"I agreed with Luke because he lined it up," Ramona explains.

"What did he line up?"

"The places."

Shannon turns to Luke, "When you were lining it up, what were you mindful of?"

"Putting the hundreds with the hundreds and the thousands, well, there was only one thousand."

Ramona adds, "And in Marin's, she put everything in the thousands."

"Oh," Marin nods and rushes up to revise her work.

"I helped her change her thinking," Ramona says.

"A lot," Marin agrees.

"And what are you thinking now?" Ms. Umberger asks Marin as she reworks the problem on the board.

"How you set up the problem makes a difference."

During this few minutes of whole-group discussion at the board, Ms. Umberger gathered a lot of data about her students: most understand the importance of lining up place value in addition problems; Ramona comprehends well enough to explain her thinking, and Marin just had an "aha" moment that will likely help her to remember this concept. Sometimes our evidence of student understanding is this clear; at other times, we need to dig deeply and take longer to understand what it is that students grasp and where they still need support.

Students are constantly communicating their understanding, either through their behavior, in their work, or with their voices. And teachers are constantly assessing and responding in turn. This chapter explores how, in the context of STEM workshops designed around rich tasks, we can remain vigilant and responsive to all learners' accomplishments and needs.

Assessment for Learning

ssessment starts with knowing what you want learners to understand and what that understanding will look and sound like. Think back to our definitions of understanding in Chapter 6 and the reality that we are operating on so many

Rachel Rosenberg's fifth graders end class by gathering under the whiteboard. She circles back to their learning target: "Who can tell us what today's main idea was?"

"The main idea of today's learning is finding ways to find the volume," Ronald explains.

"I love how you said that in a complete sentence," Rachel says. "What did you learn about volume?"

Ronald continues, "What I learned about volume is that length times width equals the base, and base times height equals the volume."

Alexia shares next, "The main idea I had today ties in to Ronald's: take the total base area and multiply it by the height. Use clues from the text to find length and width."

"And how did that help you?" Rachel prods.

levels—communicating content, teaching practices, developing identities—all within the context of a constructivist community of learners. There is a lot of intention and a lot one could attend to in this context.

In assessment for learning in any content area, we need to do the following:

- Establish and communicate clear learning targets in student-friendly language. The minilesson is an ideal time for this communication, and many teachers highlight learning targets by posting them in the classroom.

- Provide feedback to students about their understanding. Individualized feedback can be provided orally during conferring, or on written work.

- Encourage student self-assessment. The reflection component of any workshop, as described in Chapter 8, is a key time for student self-assessment in light of the learning targets. The sidebar illustrates another example.

- Monitor learning using formal and informal data. For STEM learners, this could include teacher observation, oral responses, projects, notebooks, or other artifacts and might be documented with photographs.

- Plan engaging summative assessments that create opportunities for students to share their learning with peers, parents, and others. Often "assessment" can be a euphemism for test, yet for STEM learners, demonstrations of understanding might also include inventions, presentations, lab reports, models, performances, posters, slide shows, and a wide variety of other options.

Conferring: Listening for Understanding

Conferring is a key opportunity to provoke deeper student thinking, provide individualized feedback, insert individualized instruction, and elevate STEM identity. The excitement of a busy classroom can lure us into playing the teacher role with a series of "praise, prompt, and leave" interactions. While this sort of teacher behavior can nudge all the young engineers in our care to keep busy during their work time, it is better still when we see our role as provocateur rather than police officer.

To confer is to get down eye to eye with a child and really listen to, then challenge, their thinking. This can be difficult to do given the competing needs in a classroom and our own sense that our job is to keep everyone engaged and learning. Yet, actually, it is the learners' job to take charge of themselves and to be accountable for making good choices during learning time. Once students internalize this responsibility, we are freed to become a responsive inquirer, observing and inviting rich thinking while students are deeply engaged in problem solving.

Often when we lean in, young students pepper us with questions: Is this right? How do I do this? Why does this work? Can I use the bathroom? We can be tempted to see our role as answer givers, and yet more thinking is generated when we instead respond to their questions with deeper invitations for inquiry (Figure 9.2).

Sometimes learners who may have already become accustomed to perceiving teachers as answer givers and solution blessers can become frustrated when we switch up our interactions with them. In some schools where I have worked, children have gone home reporting that their teacher was "Not teaching them," prompting calls to the administrators inquiring as to why. Parent education opportunity. The good news is that when we respond to learners' questions with questions of our own, we place the responsibility for learning squarely on their shoulders, where it belongs.

Figure 9.2 Responding to student questions with questions

When a child says . . .	Invite their thinking with . . .
Is this right?	Hmm. What do you think?
How do I do this?	What do you already know about how to begin?
Why does this work?	What a great question! How will you figure that out?
Can I use the bathroom?	Is now a good time for that, considering your responsibilities today as a learner?

Assessing While Conferring

While conferring has multiple purposes, one is assessment. To this end, it can be helpful to have a specific learning target in mind as you kneel down to confer, and to seek evidence of and document student proficiency. Some teachers travel with a clipboard holding a class list, a map of the classroom, or other graphic organizers that help them to record quickly while visiting and talking with learners in action. Confer with something to write on and write with. Note where students are and what they need next, as in Figure 9.3. Rather than trying to get to everyone every day, target engaging a few learners in meaningful conversations each day, and across a week you will reach them all.

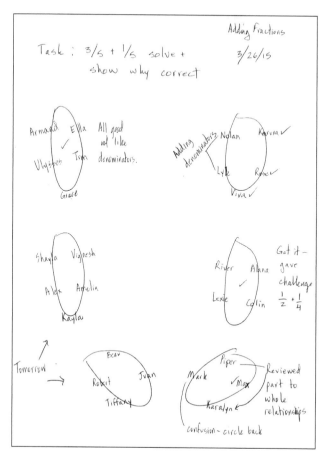

Figure 9.3 Sample Conferring Log

Notebooking: Documenting Thinking

A science notebook, field journal, engineering log, or the like is a traditional tool of a professional in a STEM field: a place to record thinking. Check out da Vinci's sketches and Darwin's logs online—scientists have always kept copious notes and careful records of their evolving understanding. Invite your students to do the same.

While students are deeply engaged in building or observing or calculating, you may feel reluctant to stop their work in order to invite documentation—and for good reasons—yet recording what they are doing and understanding is a critical step in students' STEM learning. Some teachers have even found that reluctant writers can't keep their pencils sharp enough when it comes to sketching their engineering creations or documenting their innovative calculations. STEM inspires writers.

While the lure of technology may tempt us to have students record their STEM work on a tablet or laptop, good old-fashioned pencil and paper also have their place. A field journal, math notebook, or STEM learning log can serve learners as a place to record their thinking as it grows. Some teachers will create and offer students a new packet or log for each unit or topic, while others may create a record learners can use all year long. Whatever format you choose to use, here are a few insights from experienced STEM teachers:

- Make cool covers. Rachel Rosenberg invites her students to draw themselves as scientists each year, and these self-portraits become the covers of their science notebooks, a personalized celebration of their STEM identities.

- Promote efficiency and organization by prefabbing. Instead of asking students to write everything themselves, you can either create a notebook with some prepared tables or graphic organizers specific to your unit, or give learners those pages to glue into their notebooks as needed. Some teachers will print out questions or instructions on labels, so that each child can stick one into their notebook, again saving time.

- Create a common format. When learners know how to write in their notebooks they are efficient in following that procedure. Notebooking can be modeled, and peer examples critiqued at the document camera to reinforce expectations for quality (Figure 9.4).

- Use the notebook regularly. If students are in a daily rhythm of writing in their notebooks, they will build their stamina and confidence as recorders of thinking. One teacher found that in the fall, all her students whined when asked to write about their math work, but by the end of the year they complained that seven minutes of sustained writing about math was not long enough!

- Store the notebooks in the classroom. If students' notebooks stay with you, you limit the common problem of one going missing. Even so, invariably someone's will, so have a backup plan, an extra on hand.

- Invite multimodal recording. Some entries may include labeled drawings, graphs, tables, narrative, word splashes, and so forth. For each, demonstrate for learners what their work might look like, and offer opportunities for students to explore that genre with a number of examples.

- Use tabs to separate sections. When using commercially produced

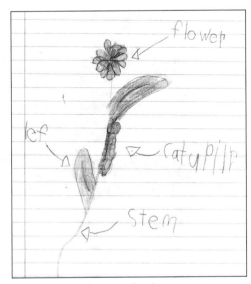

Figure 9.4 Student Notebook

composition books (which can be found with graph paper pages), it is often helpful for students to section those off so they know where each unit starts and ends. Sticky notes or adhesive tabs can serve this purpose.

- Encourage referring back to and annotating past work. Some teachers will have students glue important information into the front of their notebooks—thinking strategies, science and engineering practices, and more—for easy and regular access. Learners can also be encouraged to look back at old work or reflections on an essential question in order to build on their prior knowledge.

Assessing Notebooks

A class set of notebooks can be a lot to look through, and for some teachers is even a deterrent to creating such a system. Here are some ways to make managing notebooks easier:

- Have students mark the page you will be looking at with a paper clip, binder clip, or sticky note so that you can quickly flip to it.

- Keep them in the classroom; use a few minutes of your lunch or planning to respond to a few at a time. Don't try to carry them home, and avoid plowing through a class set all at once.

- Know what you will be looking for, and give targeted feedback on just one or two things—the content, the format, the sketch, or any other aspect that is integral to that learning experience's process target.

- Invite learners to revise their notebook entries in light of your feedback so they can be truly reflective.

Teachers who use notebooks as a place to document and celebrate thinking find that students come to take great pride in these self-created resources. Still, the perennial question recurs: grading. How do we assess them? I suggest that you use your notebooks simply as a place to hold thinking, a source of formative assessment data, but not a final product to "grade."

STEM Writing

When learners have authentic reasons to write and interesting experiences to write about, the work can come easily. Emphasize writing as an opportunity to document and share what we know. While some teachers swear by sentence starters, those can also be detrimental, since we might end up with page after page of formulaic writing and a class full of kids who hesitate to start a sentence without our handing over the first three words.

STEM writing can include lists, sketches, models, graphs, calculations, or diagrams. Check out a recent science periodical like *New Scientist* to get a flavor of how STEM professionals convey all they know. Support students in presenting their understanding in all these formats, as appropriate to their age and your content. You can show them models or exemplars—those of professionals, past students and peers—to invite discussion about what writing as scientists or mathematicians might look like. Think genre study. Students also benefit from observing you in the act of formulating your own writing before their very eyes. Think writers' workshop.

Quick Tickets

While learners may record their daily work in notebooks, on handouts, or other places, sometimes as teachers we just need to know where students stand in their understanding. For this purpose, you might use a quick ticket: a quarter or half sheet of paper with space to respond to one specific prompt or problem in writing or drawing. For example, after a workshop on building bridges, you might ask students to sketch and label the next iteration of their bridge; or, after work time exploring what it means to divide fractions, you might offer students a quick error analysis task to demonstrate their understanding: "Laurie and Sathya are sharing one-eighth of a candy bar. Laurie thinks she gets one-tenth. Is she correct?"

When we collect each child's ticket, we can quickly sort—those who agree with Laurie and those who don't, those who use the term *gravity* and those who don't—and make plans to adjust the next day's instruction accordingly.

Crosscutting Concept Dice

Teacher Kris Rasmussen keeps his students on their toes making connections between their daily learning and the crosscutting concepts. He has created paper dice, with one of the concepts on each of their six sides. He invites learners to roll a die, then describe the connection between their learning that day and the concept that arrived face up. Amazing synthesis opportunity!

Assessing Projects

While conferring, or examining notebooks and other written products that offer data on individual students' progress, culminating group tasks can sometimes be difficult to assess. Learners may come to various possible solutions or outcomes and present those in myriad formats, making identifying a specific set of look-fors challenging.

Still, a rubric as a calibrator of quality can be a useful resource to students both while developing their project and reflecting on its quality. Additive rubrics in student-friendly language inform learners of our expectations, and examining samples of student work together in light of the rubric can help to solidify students' understanding of what we are looking for.

To create an additive rubric, consider what aspects of a project you want to emphasize (because you cannot cover it all) and let those be the rows. Then,

Assessing Groupwork

If they work together, how will I know who knows what? Many teachers ask this question in the face of collaborative projects. Conferring and quick tickets are two strategies for assessing individuals' understandings and contributions. You might also invite students to write their own reflections about their group's work, their role in the project, and what they learned, then to give an honest assessment of their partners' and their contributions. Most students tend to be pretty honest in such situations, and these can be opportunities to emphasize your expectation that "You are responsible for your own learning and for supporting the learning of others," as are professional scientists.

for each row, describe the attributes you want learners to include. Across the top, note that to gain an increasing number of points, a child needs to do everything in each column to the left, building toward a pinnacle of quality. In this way, we can ensure that all language in the rubric is positive and supportive, informing a learner of what she can and will do to earn points (in contrast to some commercially produced rubrics that tabulate numbers of errors and deductions—not very growth minded!). Some teachers like to use a multiplier in the column on the right, indicating that each row or category is weighted, more points for content, for example, than presentation (Figure 9.5).

A good rubric can take a few iterations to create and needs field testing in order to ensure its accuracy, yet once we develop an effective one, it can be reused year to year and sometimes project to project. Try it out. Start by envisioning your best hope for students' work, and take time to articulate how they will build toward that goal.

Figure 9.5 Sample Generic Additive Rubric

	1	3	5	Multiplier
		All of 1, plus . . .	*All of 3, plus . . .*	
Content Understanding	Uses academic language accurately	Provides ideas and examples to demonstrate understanding	Offers description, detail, and illustrations to explain	____ x 2 = ____
Process	Completes original work	Poses and responds to interesting questions	Justifies connections to Big Ideas	____ x 2 = ____
Presentation	Legible	Comprehensible	Ready to publish	____ x 1 = ____
TOTAL				

Revision

"We make mistakes; we are all learning together, we are all different learners." Michelle DuMoulin describes her philosophy on errors in first grade. "Students need to really quickly understand that we are all just different, and it's all okay. To hear that whatever they are thinking is okay is important for kids." She models every day in class the value she places on learners changing their thinking—that this is a good thing, a sign of growth. "We talk constantly about how your best learning happens when you have to change your mind."

"It's okay not to know it right now," Michelle tells students. "We are a community, and we are all in this together. We are gonna make mistakes and learn from them. We talk a lot about perseverance, my motto in everything. Really important."

To this end, allow ample opportunity for learners to revise their work in light of feedback. This is critical to their own self-awareness as well to as the cultivation of their intrinsic sense of quality.

Evidence Every Day

You are always watching, listening, reading, and interacting with learners. By virtue of the time you spend with them you are constantly gathering data on who understands what and who needs what and using that to adjust your course and make decisions about where the class will go next. Sometimes opening up student work to include notebooks, projects, models, and other problem-solving tasks can seem like it will make assessment (okay, even grading) more cumbersome. The reality is that when you know your purpose and the targets for understanding for each task, create rubrics as appropriate, and take time to document learners' contributions and ideas in a central place, you can gather ample evidence toward assessment.

Above all, as teachers, our role is to facilitate mindful STEM learning adventures; let us not get stuck in the muck of cataloguing points or assigning grades to every task. Rather, sustain a focus on promoting learners' understanding, keep an eye on evidence along those lines, and you and your students will enjoy the process of coming to know STEM, and yourselves as scientists.

CONCLUSION

So What?

Teacher Belief	Teacher Behavior	Learner Experience	Learner Identity
I can cultivate STEM identities.	Teachers experiment with the ideas in this text to transform students' STEM experiences.	STEM subjects are relevant, engaging, interesting, and worthy of the hard work they entail.	I love STEM!

Central Question: What will you do with what you know?

Our STEM identities inform our choices and define our futures. STEM identities can be intentionally cultivated with attention to beliefs, mindsets, school culture, and pedagogy. This book has offered you an array of information and suggestions along those lines. Choosing to take this knowledge and put it into action for your students can open their minds to a world of wonder as yet unseen.

Anybody can dig a hole and plant a tree. But make sure it survives. You have to nurture it, you have to water it, you have to keep at it until it becomes rooted so it can take care of itself.

—Wangari Mathai, Nobel Laureate

As you proceed, consider these possibilities:

- Talk to friends and colleagues about their STEM identities and how those impacted their lives.

- Ponder your STEM beliefs and those posed in the text. Thinking about what you hold dear to your heart and how to enact those beliefs for learners will fuel your work.

- Level with your students about what you know and understand about the importance of STEM identity and the intentional ways it can be cultivated.

Stop and Think

- How do you want learners to think of themselves as scientists and mathematicians?

- To that end, what is most important?

- Create worthy learning experiences that demand thinking and collaboration; dwell in the struggle right alongside learners.

- Celebrate understanding and perseverance, both in yourself and in your students.

- Keep the faith. Change is hard. Take your time. We are working against thousands of years of societies that relegated certain roles and bodies of knowledge to certain individuals based on their status, gender, race, or religion.

- Trust yourself. Whatever you do to intentionally promote STEM identities is a gift to your students. Give what you can.

While working on this book, I have raised the topic of STEM identity with a broad constellation of folks. As I shared research and listened to stories, I found out that nearly

everyone, including smart, successful STEM professionals, has a unique STEM identity experience, often one involving challenge and struggle: math anxiety in second grade, girls not being allowed into the computer lab at lunch in middle school, a racist chemistry teacher in high school, a college counselor who tried to advise a keen learner out of applying to medical school. Early STEM experiences, unfortunate or encouraging, shape us and mold our futures.

We have an opportunity to write for children of all backgrounds, genders, and races a new story about what STEM is and who belongs in these fields, to ensure that everyone cultivates STEM identities.

Favorite STEM Read-Alouds

Aston, Sylvia Hutts. *An Egg Is Quiet.*

Aston, Sylvia Hutts. *A Nest Is Noisy.*

Aston, Sylvia Hutts. *A Rock Is Lively.*

Aston, Sylvia Hutts. *A Seed Is Sleepy.*

Beaty, Andrea. *Rosie Revere, Engineer.*

Berne, Jennifer. *On a Beam of Light: A Story of Albert Einstein.*

D'Agnese, Joseph. *Blockhead: The Life of Fibonacci.*

Davies, Jacqueline. *The Boy Who Drew Birds: A Story of John James Audobon.*

Demi. *One Grain of Rice: A Mathematical Folktale.*

Fleming, Candace. *Papa's Mechanical Fish.*

Heiligman, Deborah. *The Boy Who Loved Math: The Improbable Life of Paul Erdos.*

Hopkins, H. Joseph. *The Tree Lady: The True Story of How One Tree-Loving Woman Changed a City Forever.*

Lasky, Kathryn. *The Librarian Who Measured the Earth.*

Lehn, Barbara. *What Is a Scientist?*

McCully, Emily Arnold. *Marvelous Mattie: How Margaret E. Knight Became an Inventor.*

McDonnell, Patrick. *Me . . . Jane.*

Nivola, Claire A. *Planting the Trees of Kenya: The Story of Wangari Maathai.*

Scieszka, Jon. *Math Curse.*

Scieszka, Jon. *Science Verse.*

Sharafeddine, Fatima. *The Amazing Discoveries of Ibn Sina.*

Sis, Peter. *Starry Messenger: Galileo Galilei.*

Sisson, Stephanie Roth. *Star Stuff: Carl Sagan and the Mysteries of the Cosmos.*

Smith, David J. *If: A Mind-Bending New Way of Looking at Big Ideas and Numbers.*

Wallmark, Laurie. *Ada Byron Lovelace and the Thinking Machine.*

Yamada, Kobi. *What Do You Do with an Idea?*

Favorite STEM Songs

"Count on Me" by Bruno Mars

"Expanding Universe" by Dana Lyons

"Seasons of Love (525,600 Minutes)" from "Rent"

"We Can Work It Out" by The Beatles

The entire *School House Rock—Multiplication Rock* album

The entire *They Might Be Giants—Science Is Real* album

Favorite STEM Resources

Alltop—Top Math News
http://math.alltop.com

Estimation 180
www.estimation180.com

Kids Discover
www.kidsdiscover.com/shop/?gclid=Cj0KEQiAhuSzBRDBoZfG56bK9-YBEiQARiPcZ
atoEx9AKzgQpFEdEijSW0B_6L9PDkiok6vHAGJGNL8aArZd8P8HAQ

Kodo Kids
http://kodokids.com

Math—Light Years—CNN.com Blogs
http://lightyears.blogs.cnn.com/category/on-earth/math/

New Scientist
www.newscientist.com

Newsela
https://newsela.com

Science Friday, NPR
www.sciencefriday.com

You Cubed
www.youcubed.org

Yummy Math
www.yummymath.com

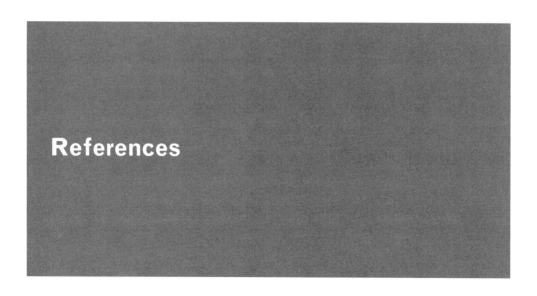

References

100Kin10. 2015. "Grand Challenges." https://100kin10.org/news/100kin10-leads-innovative-effort-to-name-the-grand-challenges-in-stem-teaching?

Achieve, Inc. 2013. "The Next Generation Science Standards." Retrieved October 7 from www.nextgenscience.org/next-generation-science-standards.

American Association for the Advancement of Science Education. 1989. "Project 2061." *Science for All Americans.* New York: Oxford University Press.

———. 1993. *Benchmarks for Science Literacy.* New York: Oxford University Press.

Andrus, Miranda R., and Mary T. Roth. 2002. "Health Literacy: A Review." *Pharmacotherapy* 22 (3 II): 282–302.

Beery, Annaliese K., and Irving Zucker. 2011. "Sex Bias in Neuroscience and Biomedical Research." *Neuroscience & Behavioral Reviews* 35 (3): 565–72.

Bennett, Samantha. 2007. *That Workshop Book.* Portsmouth, NH: Heinemann.

Bielock, Sian, Elizabeth A. Gunderson, Gerardo Ramirez, and Susan C. Levine. 2010. "Female Teachers' Math Anxiety Affects Girls' Math Achievement." Proceedings of the National Academy of Sciences, January 11. 107 (5).

Blackwell, Lisa S., Kali H. Trzesniewski, and Carol S. Dweck. 2007. "Implicit Theories of Intelligence Predict Achievement Across an Adolescent Transition: A Longitudinal Study and an Intervention." *Child Development* 78 (1): 246–63.

Boaler, Jo. 2006. "How a Detracked Mathematics Approach Promoted Respect, Responsibility, and High Achievement." *Theory into Practice* 45 (1): 40.

———. 2013. "The Sterotypes That Distort How Americans Teach and Learn Math." *The Atlantic*, November 12. www.theatlantic.com/education/archive/2013/11/the-stereotypes-that-distort-how-americans-teach-and-learn-math/281303/.

———. 2015a. "Fluency Without Fear: Research Evidence on the Best Way to Learn Math Facts." *youcubed* January 28. www.youcubed.org/fluency-without-fear/.

———. 2015b. 'Memorizers and the Lowest Achievers and Other Common Core Math Surprises." *The Hechinger Report*. May 7. http://hechingerreport.org/memorizers-are-the-lowest-achievers-and-other-common-core-math-surprises/.

Bronson, Po and Ashley Merryman. 2010. "The Creativity Crisis." *Newsweek*, July 10. www.newsweek.com/creativity-crisis-74665.

Bryson, Bill. 2003. *A Short History of Nearly Everything*. New York: Broadway Books.

Ceci, S. J., W. M. Williams, and S. M. Barnett. 2009. "Women's Underrepresentation in Science: Sociocultural and Biological Considerations." *Psychological Bulletin* 135 (2): 218–261.

Chapin, Suzanne H., Mary Catherine O'Connor, and Nancy Canavan Anderson. 2009. *Classroom Discussions: Using Math Talk to Help Students Learn, Grades K–6*. Sausalito, CA: Math Solutions.

Charles, Randall. 2005. "Big Ideas and Understandings as the Foundation for Elementary and Middle School Mathematics." *Journal of Mathematics Education Leadership* 7 (3): 9–24.

Chase, W. G., and H. A. Simon. 1973. "The Minds Eye In Chess." In *Visual Information Processing*, edited by W. G. Chase. New York: Academic Press.

Chi, Michelene T. H., Nicholas De Leeuw, Mei-Hung H. Chiu, and Christian LaVancher. 1994. "Eliciting Self-Explanations Improves Understanding." *Cognitive Science* 18 (3): 439–77.

Clements, Douglas H., and Julie Sarama. 2011. "Early Childhood Mathematics Intervention." *Science* 333 (6045): 968–70.

Clifford, M. M., and F. C. Chou. 1991. "Effects of Payoff and Task Context on Academic Risk Taking." *Journal of Educational Psychology* 83 (4): 499–507.

Cohen, E. G., and R. A. Lotan. 1997. *Working for Equity in Heterogeneous Classrooms: Sociological Theory into Practice*. New York: Teachers College Press.

Committee on STEM Education, National Science and Technology Council. 2013. *Federal Science, Technology, Engineering and Mathematics (STEM) Education Five Year Strategic Plan*. Washington, D.C.: Executive Office of the President of the United States. www.whitehouse.gov/sites/default/files/microsites/ostp/stem_stratplan_2013.pdf

Common Core State Standards Initiative. 2010. *Common Core State Standards for Mathematics*. Retrieved from www.corestandards.org/assets/CCSSI_Math%20Standards.pdf.

Covey, Stephen. 2004. *The 7 Habits of Highly Effective People*. New York: Simon & Schuster.

CTEq. 2012. *Vital Signs: Reports on the Condition of STEM Learning in the U.S.* Washington, DC: Change the Equation. Retrieved from http://changetheequation.org/sites/default/files/CTEq_VitalSigns_Supply%20%282%29.pdf.

Cvencek, Dario, Andrew N. Meltzoff, and Anthony G. Greenwald. 2011. "Math-Gender Stereotypes in Elementary School Children." *Child Development*: 1–14.

Delpit, Lisa. 2012. *"Multiplication Is for White People": Raising Expectations for Other People's Children*. New York: The New Press.

Desert, Michael, Marie Preaux, and Robin Jund. 2009. "So Young and Already Victims of Stereotype Threat: Socio-Economic Status and Performance of 6 to 9 Years Old Children on Raven's Progressive Matrices." *European Journal of Psychology of Education* 24 (2): 207–18.

Dreifus, Claudia. 2013. "Ideas for Improving Science Education." *New York Times*, September 2.

Duncan, Greg J., Chantelle J. Dowsett, Amy Claessens, Katherine Magnuson, Aletha C. Huston, Pamela Klebanov, Linda S. Pagani, Leon Feinstein, Mimi Engel, Jeanne Brooks-Gunn, Holly Sexton, Kathryn Duckworth, and Crista Japel. 2007. "School Readiness and Later Achievement." *Developmental Psychology* 43 (6): 1428–1446.

Dweck, Carol. 2006. *Mindset: The New Psychology of Success*. New York: Random House.

Fleischman, Howard L., Paul J. Hopstock, Marisa P. Pelczar, and Brooke E. Shelley. 2010. "Highlights from PISA 2009: Performance of US 15-Year-Old Students in Reading, Mathematics, and Science Literacy in an International Context." NCES 2011-004. National Center for Education Statistics. Retrieved from www.eric.ed.gov/ERICWebPortal/recordDetail?accno=ED513640.

Gardinier, Tom. 2014. "Cosmos Interview with Ann Druyan and Neil deGrasse Tyson." www.threeifbyspace.net/2014/03/cosmos-interview-with-ann-druyan-and-neil-degrasse-tyson/#.VpRIY0u7Ids.

Goodall, Jane. 1999. *Reason for Hope*. New York: Soko.

Graves, Donald. 1983. *Writing: Teachers and Students at Work*. Portsmouth, NH: Heinemann.

Hanushek, Erik A., Paul E. Peterson, and Ludger Woessmann. 2012. *Achievement Growth: International and U.S. State Trends in Student Performance*. Harvard's Program on Education Policy and Governance.

Hattie, John. 2009. *Visible Learning: A Synthesis of Over 800 Meta-Analyses Relating to Achievement*. London: Routledge.

Hattie, John, and Helen Timperley. 2007. "The Power of Feedback." *Review of Educational Research* 77 (1): 81–112.

Herr, Norman. 2007. "How Two Experts Differ from Novices." Internet Resources to Accompany *The Sourcebook for Teaching Science*. California State University, Northridge. www.csun.edu/science/ref/reasoning/how-students-learn/2.html.

Hiebert, James. 1997. *Making Sense: Teaching and Learning Mathematics with Understanding*. Portsmouth, NH: Heinemann.

Hoffer, Wendy Ward. 2009. *Science as Thinking: The Constants and Variables of Inquiry Teaching, Grades 5–10*. Portsmouth, NH: Heinemann.

——. 2012. *Minds on Mathematics: Using Math Workshop to Develop Deep Understanding in Grades 4–8*. Portsmouth, NH: Heinemann.

——. 2016. *Developing Literate Mathematicians: A Guide for Integrating Language and Literacy Instruction into Secondary Mathematics*. Reston, VA: National Council of Teachers of Mathematics.

Holt, John. 1995. *How Children Learn*. Boston: De Capo Press.

Jahren, Hope. 2016. *Lab Girl*. New York: Alfred A. Knopf.

Johnston, Peter H. 2004. *Choice Words: How Our Language Affects Children's Learning*. Portland, ME: Stenhouse.

——. 2012. *Opening Minds: Using Language to Change Lives*. Portland, ME: Stenhouse.

Kahn, Albert. 1970. *Joys and Sorrows: Reflections of Pablo Casals*. New York: Simon & Schuster.

Keene, Ellin Oliver. 2008. *To Understand: New Horizons in Reading Comprehension*. Portsmouth, NH: Heinemann.

Keene, Ellin Oliver and Susan Zimmermann. 1997. *Mosaic of Thought*. Portsmouth, NH: Heinemann.

Knapton, Sarah. 2015. "Sir Tim Hunt Deserved to Lose His Job over 'Chauvinist' Comments, Nobel Prize Winner Says." *The Telegraph*, July 10. www.telegraph.co.uk/news/science/science-news/11732143/Sir-Tim-Hunt-deserved-to-lose-his-job-over-chauvinist-comments-Nobel-Prize-winner-says.html.

Kohn, Alfie. 1999. *Punished by Rewards: The Trouble with Gold Stars, Incentive Plans, A'S, Praise and Other Bribes*. Boston: Houghton Mifflin.

Kolb, David A. 1984. *Experiential Learning: Experience as the Source of Learning and Development*. Vol. 1. Englewood Cliffs, NJ: Prentice-Hall.

Langdon, David, George McKittrick, David Beede, Beethika Khan, and Mark Doms. 2011. *STEM: Good Jobs Now and for the Future*. ESA Issue Brief #03-11. Washington, DC: U.S. Department of Commerce.

Lavy, Victor, and Edith Sand. 2015. "On the Origins of Gender Human Capital Gaps: Short and Long Term Consequences of Teachers' Stereotypical Biases." NBER Working Paper No. w20909. January. Available at SSRN: http://ssrn.com/abstract=2558961.

McLain, Bradley. 2012. "Science Identity Construction Through Extraordinary Professional Development Experiences." Doctoral thesis, University of Colorado. Available at: http://digitool.library.colostate.edu///exlibris/dtl/d3_1/apache_media/L2V4bGlicmlzL2R0bC9kM18xL2FwYWNoZV9tZWRpYS8xNzUwMTE=.pdf.

Market Research Institute. 2004. *The Bayer Facts of Science Education X Survey: Are the Nation's Colleges and Universities Adequately Preparing Elementary Schoolteachers of Tomorrow to Teach Science?* http://hub.mspnet.org/index.cfm/9489.

Mathai, Wangari. 2008. "This Much I Know." *The Guardian*. June 7. www.theguardian.com/environment/2008/jun/08/2.

Medina, John. 2015. "Brain Rules for Presenters." Accessed at: http://us8.campaign-archive2 .com/?u=e727fa52c1ad06a6270c45363&id=c8de0a7388&e=c1d79f67b1.

Metz, B. K. E. 2008. "Narrowing the Gulf Between the Practices of Science and the Elementary School Science Classroom." *The Elementary School Journal* 109 (2): 138–61. doi:10.1086/595725.

Michaels, Sarah, Catherine O'Connor, and Lauren Resnick. 2008. "Reasoned Participation: Accountable Talk in the Classroom and in Civic Life." *Studies in Philosophy and Education* 27 (4): 283–97.

Mitchell, Gareth. 2013. "How Many Terabytes of Data Are on the Internet?" Science Focus. *BBC Focus* online, January 23. www.sciencefocus.com/qa/how-many-terabytes-data-are -internet.

Mueller, Claudia M., and Carol S. Dweck. 1998. "Praise for Intelligence Can Undermine Children's Motivation and Performance." *Journal of Personality and Social Psychology* 75 (33–52).

National Academy of Sciences. 2007. *Beyond Bias and Barriers: Fulfilling the Potential of Women in Academic Science and Engineering.* Washington, DC: National Academies Press.

National Council of Teachers of Mathematics. 1998. *Principles and Standards for School Mathematics.* Reston, VA: National Council of Teachers of Mathematics.

———. 2014. *Principles to Actions: Ensuring Mathematical Success for All.* Reston, VA: National Council of Teachers of Mathematics.

National Girls Collaborative Project. 2015. "The State of Girls and Women in STEM." www .ngcproject.org/statistics.

National Research Council. 1996. *National Science Education Standards.* Washington, DC: National Academies Press.

———. 2000. *How People Learn.* Washington, DC: National Academies Press.

———. 2001. *Adding It Up: Helping Children Learn Mathematics.* Washington, DC: National Academies Press.

———. 2012. *A Framework for K–12 Science Education: Practices, Crosscutting Concepts, and Core Ideas.* Committee on a Conceptual Framework for New K–12 Science Education Standards. Board on Science Education, Division of Behavioral and Social Sciences and Education. Washington, DC: The National Academies Press.

———. 2013. "Appendix G: Crosscutting Concepts." www.nextgenscience.org/sites/ngss/files/ Appendix%20G%20-%20Crosscutting%20Concepts%20FINAL%20edited%204.10.13.pdf.

National Science Foundation, National Center for Science and Engineering Statistics. 2013. "Women, Minorities, and Persons with Disabilities in Science and Engineering: 2013." Special Report NSF 13-304. Arlington, Virginia. Available at www.nsf.gov/statistics/wmpd/.

Niemi, David, Julia Vallone, and Terry Vendlinski. 2006. "The Power of Big Ideas in Mathematics Education: Development and Pilot Testing of POWERSOURCE Assessments." National Center for Research on Evaluation, Standards, and Student Testing (CRESST), Center for the

Study of Evaluation (CSE), Graduate School of Education & Information Studies University of California, Los Angeles. http://files.eric.ed.gov/fulltext/ED494280.pdf.

OECD. 2009. *PISA 2009 Assessment Framework: Key Competencies in Reading, Mathematics and Science*. Paris: OECD.

———. 2010. *PISA 2009 at a Glance*. http://dx.doi.org/10.1787/9789264095298-en.

Osborne, Jonathan, Shirley Simon, and Susan Collins. 2003. "Attitudes Toward Science: A Review of the Literature." *International Journal of Science Education* 25 (9): 1049–79.

Pearson, P. David, and Margaret Gallagher. 1983. *The Instruction of Reading Comprehension*. Champaign: University of Illinois at Urbana-Champaign.

———. "The Instruction of Reading Comprehension." *Contemporary Educational Psychology* 8: 317–44.

Pearson, P. David, Laura R. Roehler, Janice A. Dole, and Gerald G. Duffy. 1992. "Developing Expertise in Reading Comprehension: What Should Be Taught and Who Should Teach It." In *What Research Has to Say About Reading Instruction*, 2d ed., edited by Jay Samuels and Alan Farstrup. Newark, DE: International Reading Association.

Poincare, Henri. 1905. *Science and Hypothesis*. London: Walter Scott.

President's Council of Advisors on Science and Technology. 2012. *Engage to Excel: Producing One Million Additional College Graduates with Degrees in Science, Technology, Engineering, and Mathematics*. Report to the President. Executive Office of the President. Retrieved from www.eric.ed.gov/ERICWebPortal/recordDetail?accno=ED541511.

Prince, Michael. 2004. "Does Active Learning Work? A Review of the Research." *Journal of Engineering Education* 93 (3): 223–231. doi:10.1002/j.2168-9830.2004.tb00809.x.

Provasnik, Steven., David Kastberg, David Ferraro, Nita Lemanski, Stephen Roey, and Frank Jenkins. 2012. "Highlights from TIMSS 2011: Mathematics and Science Achievement of US Fourth-and Eighth-Grade Students in an International Context." NCES 2013-009. *National Center for Education Statistics*. Retrieved from www.eric.ed.gov/ERICWebPortal/recordDetail?accno=ED537756.

Robert Wood Johnson Foundation. 2011. "Study Shows Need to Eliminate Sex Bias in Research." http://vcresearch.berkeley.edu/news/study-shows-need-eliminate-sex-bias-research.

Rowe, Mary Budd. 1986. "Wait Time: Slowing Down May Be a Way of Speeding Up." *Journal of Teacher Education*. January (37) 1; 43–50.

Sagan, Carl. 1994. *Pale Blue Dot: A Vision of the Human Future in Space*. New York: Random House.

Sampson, Scott. 2014. Address to PEBC STEM Summit, May 5. Museum of Nature and Science, Denver, CO.

Schoenfeld, Alan, and Deborah Stipek. 2011. *Math Matters: Children's Mathematical Journeys Start Early*. Conference Report, www.earlylearning.org.

Schwartz, Katrina. 2014. "What's Your Learning Disposition? How to Foster Students' Mindsets." Mind/Shift. http://blogs.kqed.org/mindshift/2014/03/whats-your-learning-disposition-how-to-foster-students-mindsets/.

Sparks, Sarah. 2015. "Positive Mindset May Prime Students' Brains for Math." *Education Week*, December 8.

Spiegel, Alix. 2012. "Struggle for Smarts? How Eastern and Western Cultures Tackle Learning." Retrieved from www.npr.org/blogs/health/2012/11/12/164793058/struggle-for-smarts-how-eastern-and-western-cultures-tackle-learning.

Stigler, James, Ronald Gallimore, and James Hiebert. 2000. "Using Video Surveys to Compare Classrooms and Teaching Across Cultures: Examples and Lessons from the TIMSS Video Studies." *Educational Psychologist* 35 (2): 87–100.

Sullivan, Patricia. 2009. "Jerri Nielsen; Doctor Battled Cancer at South Pole." *The Washington Post*, June 26. www.washingtonpost.com/wp-dyn/content/article/2009/06/24/AR2009062403094.html.

Tennessee Department of Education. 2014. "Illuminating Student Thinking: Assessing and Advancing Questions." Retrieved from www.tncore.org/sites/www/Uploads/files/K_2_training/Tab5a_Assess_Advance_Slides_NOTES.pdf.

University of Chicago. 2010. "Believing Stereotype Undermines Girls' Math Performance: Elementary School Women Teachers Transfer Their Fear of Doing Math to Girls, Study Finds." *ScienceDaily*. 26 January. www.sciencedaily.com/releases/2010/01/100125172940.htm.

U.S. Department of Health and Human Services. 2015. "Quick Guide to Health Literacy." http://health.gov/communication/literacy/quickguide/factsbasic.htm.

Vygotsky, Lev S. 1978. *Mind in Society: The Development of Higher Mental Process*. Cambridge, MA: Harvard University Press.

Weinburgh, M. H. 1998. "Middle School Students' Grade Expectation and Preferred Topics in Science by Gender and Ethnicity." *Current Issues in Middle Level Education*, 7 (2): 74–88.

Wertheimer, Max. 1959. *Productive Thinking*. New York: Harper and Row.

White House Office of Science and Technology Policy. 2013. "Preparing a 21st Century Workforce: Science, Technology, Engineering, and Mathematics (STEM) Education in the 2014 Budget." Washington, D.C. Retrieved from www.whitehouse.gov/sites/default/files/microsites/ostp/2014_R&Dbudget_STEM.pdf.

Wiggins, Grant, and Jay McTighe. 1998. *Understanding by Design*. Alexandria, VA: ASCD.

Zwiers, Jeff, Susan O'Hara, and Robert Henry Pritchard. 2014. *Common Core Standards in Diverse Classrooms: Essential Practices for Developing Academic Language and Disciplinary Literacy*. Portland, ME: Stenhouse.